Contents

D0515017

In the morning, the farmer again made his way through the castle. Still he found no one to whom he could give his grateful thanks. At last, he gave up the search and went out to saddle his horse. As he walked out into the sunshine, he saw a profusion of roses in the garden. The flowers were **fragrant** and lovely and reminded him of Beauty's simple request.

Happily, the farmer took a small knife from his pocket and cut the stem of a single red rose. At once, he heard a loud roar.

He looked up to see a large, frightening beast bounding across the garden. The beast had sharp teeth and fierce claws. His face was terrible to behold. The farmer shook with fear as the beast came to a stop right in front of him.

"I give you food and shelter, and this is how you repay me?" shouted the beast. "I offer you my hospitality, and in turn you steal from me! Perhaps I should tear you limb from limb!"

With a trembling voice, the farmer tried to explain. "Please forgive me. I did not mean to steal from you. I took the rose for my kind and lovely daughter. She is a good girl and helps me in every way. She asked me to bring her a rose, and I only thought to make her happy."

The beast growled. "Hmm. Your daughter sounds like a devoted and beautiful young woman."

"Yes, in every way," agreed the farmer. "Please do not kill me. If I die, my poor Beauty and her sisters will be orphans. Have mercy, I beg you."

"All right," said the beast, grudgingly. "I shall spare your life. But only on one condition. In three days, you must return with your daughter. She must come to live with me. If you do not return, I shall hunt you down and kill you. Do not forget!"

The beast bounded away into the woods. Sadly, the farmer mounted his horse and rode home. When he told his daughters what had happened, Brinna and Flona began to cry and scream hysterically. But Beauty hugged her father close. "Of course, I will go," she said calmly. "There is no choice."

Beauty
and the
Beast

Once upon a time, a long time ago, there lived a farmer named Sebastian and his three daughters. The family lived in the country in a snug little house. They were far from **wealthy**, but they had plenty of food, warm clothes, and a good life. This was not enough for the two older daughters, Brinna and Flona. These two were always sighing and complaining. They were never happy with what they had, but were always wanting more. They longed for golden rings to put on their fingers and for strings of pearls to wear around their necks. They did not like their soft cotton **frocks** and begged their father for silk dresses to wear. But their father would simply shake his head and laugh at their demands.

"Foolish girls," he would say. "You know we cannot afford such **folly**."

But the youngest daughter was different. Her name was Beauty. Beauty liked to help her father with the family's chores. She was gifted at caring for the animals, and always had a fine flock of fat geese and plump chickens. The garden she tended produced delicious vegetables and lovely flowers. Beauty was always singing and smiling as she went about her work. She never asked for anything, and was very content.

One day, the father gathered his three daughters and told them he was planning to make his once-a-year trip to the distant city to buy the things they would need in the months to come. He asked each of his daughters to name some small gift he might purchase for them in the city. Brinna demanded a ruby-encrusted bracelet. Flona tossed her head and said, "I want a pair of gold slippers."

Their father sighed, and shook his head in disgust at these **extravagant** requests. But Beauty touched her father's arm and said softly, "I would like a rose, Father. That is the only flower that does not grow in my garden."

"Oh, Beauty, you're a fine girl," said her father, smiling again. With a fond wave for Beauty and a frown for Brinna and Flona, he set off for the city.

In the city, the farmer went about his business. He bought seed for the next year's crop, nails for the horse's shoes, shingles to repair the barn roof, and paint to freshen the old house. His errands took a long time, and the hour grew late. By the time Sebastian had finished his shopping, evening shadows were beginning to stretch across the countryside. In spite of the gathering gloom, Sebastian decided to start toward home.

As he hurried along the path, the night grew darker and darker. Clouds cove the moon. With no light at all to guide him, Sebastian became lost in the woods He was beginning to feel very tired and more than a bit frightened when he spic a light shining through the trees. He turned his tired horse's head toward the lig As they drew closer, the farmer saw the outlines of a large castle. Through an o doorway, light spilled into the courtyard.

The farmer drew his horse to a stop in front of the castle. Entering the open doorway, he called out. But no one answered. The farmer stepped inside and cal again. Still, no one answered. As he looked around, he noticed that a lovely table stood in the center of the room. The table was laid with fine linens and lit with several glowing candles. Enormous bowls and platters of steaming food covered the table. A single gold plate sat empty and waiting.

The farmer was very hungry after his long day. He felt a bit uncomfortable about making himself at home in this strange place, but his belly growled and the food **beckoned**. So he sat down and ate his fill. When he had finished, the farmer walked through the rooms of the castle, looking for his host. But he saw no one. In one of the rooms, he found a soft bed covered with warm blankets and big fluffy pillows. He was so tired he could not resist. He fell into the bed and slept soundly all the night long.

When three days had passed, Beauty and her father rode back through the woods to the castle. As before, the door was open. As before, a beautiful table stood in the great hall. This time, it was set for two, with golden dishes and crystal **goblets**. Beauty and her father sat down at the table. Sebastian began to eat, but Beauty was filled with dread and could hardly swallow a **morsel**. Instead, she sat and gazed around her, amazed at the richness of her surroundings. Rich **tapestries** hung from the walls. Intricate carpets covered the floor. Candles gleamed from a golden chandelier, casting shadows into the corners of the room.

Suddenly, from within a shadowed corner, the Beast appeared and approached the table. Beauty grew tense with fear, but she forced herself to look steadily at the creature. He was fearsome indeed, just as her father had described, but Beauty noticed that his face wore a sad expression, and that his eyes seemed dull with grief.

"Welcome," said the beast as he came forward. He spoke softly and gently. "I am so glad that you have agreed to come and live here in my castle. I wish to give you everything you desire. You will be safe here. You will have anything you want, but you must never leave me. As for you," the Beast said, turning to Sebastian, "it is time for you to go."

Beauty bit her lips to hold back tears. She wanted nothing more than to go home with her father. But she knew this was not possible. "I understand, Beast," she said calmly. "I will do as you say." She kissed her father and watched him ride away, waving until he was out of sight.

The beast kept his word to Beauty, and he was unfailingly kind to her. He provided her with delicious and elaborate food to eat and expensive and beautiful clothing to wear. When she mentioned that she would like to have some books to read, he presented her with an entire room lined with thousands of volumes on every subject imaginable.

Soon, she overcame her fear of the beast and found that she enjoyed talking with him. Sometimes, happy in Beauty's company, the beast smiled and even laughed a little. But whenever she looked into his eyes, she saw the deep sadness that lay within like a pool of dark water.

Every night, as they sat together in the garden, the beast would ask Beauty to marry him. Every night, Beauty gently and sadly refused. Although she felt sorry for the Beast, she did not love him.

Things went on this way for over a year. Then one morning, Beauty picked up her mirror. Instead of her own face, she saw a vision of her father, lying sick and in pain. She flew to the Beast to tell him what she had seen. She begged permission to go to her father.

"Of course, Beauty, go to your father. But you must promise to return to me within one month. For if you do not, I shall surely die of loneliness."

Beauty raced home to find that the vision in her mirror was indeed true. Her father was very ill, and Brinna and Flona, in their selfishness, had not given him proper care. His bedding was **rumpled** and **soiled**. He was cold and hungry. Beauty quickly found clean sheets and extra blankets. She smoothed the pillow under her father's head. She made him some strengthening broth and warm gruel. Under the care of her tender hands, he slowly began to recover.

The weeks passed, and her father's health improved. But still he was weak and frail. Beauty remembered her promise to the Beast, but she was afraid to leave her father's side. Brinna and Flona, too, encouraged her to stay. They were happy to have someone there to do the cooking and cleaning, tasks they avoided at all costs. Besides, they told her again and again, "You are the only one who can make Father well."

So a month passed, and Beauty began to feel at home again with her family. Her life with the Beast began to seem like a distant dream. Then one morning, she picked up her mirror to see a new vision. There, in the glass, she saw the Beast, lying still and cold. Beauty screamed and fell to her knees in **agony**.

"Oh, it is my fault," she cried. "Poor Beast. I'm coming. Please don't die." Beauty hastily put on her cape and ran to where her father sat in the sunshine.

"Father, I must go back to the Beast. He is ill. I must hurry."

Sebastian pleaded with Beauty to stay. Brinna and Flona whined **piteously**. But Beauty would not listen. She leaped onto her horse and was off through the woods in an instant.

When she arrived at the castle, she dashed from room to room, calling for the Beast, but he did not answer. At last, she ran out into the garden, and there she found him, lying among the roses. He was so still that at first she thought he was dead. She threw herself down on the ground next to him, and laid her head on his chest. Faintly, she heard his heart beating. Faintly, she felt his breath move on her soft cheek.

 Reading • EMC 4533 • ©2005 by Evan-Moor Corp.

"Oh, you're alive!" she exclaimed with joy. "Beast, please wake up. If only you will open your eyes and be well, I promise never to leave you. I do love you, Beast. I will marry you, if only you will live!"

The Beast's eyelids fluttered. His huge hairy body stirred, and he sat up. Beauty threw her arms around his neck and hugged him tightly. As she drew back to look at him, she cried out in surprise. In the place of the Beast, there sat a handsome prince.

"Don't be afraid, Beauty," he said in the Beast's deep and familiar voice. "I am your Beast. I was enchanted by an evil fairy. I was doomed to live my life as a beast unless I could persuade someone to love me in spite of my appearance. You, Beauty, have freed me."

They fell together, laughing and crying at once in their great happiness.

So Beauty and the prince were married and lived joyfully for all their lives. Beauty brought her family to live in the castle, where her father's health and **vigor** soon returned. And although Brinna and Flona were as jealous and selfish as ever, Beauty was kind to them anyway.

Questions About
Beauty and the Beast

Fill in the circle that best answers each question.

1. Beauty asked her father to bring her _____.
   - Ⓐ a chrysanthemum
   - Ⓑ a dandelion
   - Ⓒ a daisy
   - Ⓓ a rose

2. Beauty's sisters were _____.
   - Ⓐ kind and generous
   - Ⓑ grumpy and selfish
   - Ⓒ caring and obedient
   - Ⓓ thoughtful and hardworking

3. Beauty went to live with the Beast because _____.
   - Ⓐ she wanted to live in a palace
   - Ⓑ she wanted to help her father
   - Ⓒ she was kidnapped
   - Ⓓ he was hungry

4. It seemed to Beauty that the Beast often felt _____.
   - Ⓐ happy
   - Ⓑ angry
   - Ⓒ silly
   - Ⓓ sad

5. The Beast allowed Beauty to leave him because _____.
   - Ⓐ her father was very ill
   - Ⓑ she wanted to attend school
   - Ⓒ she needed to go shopping
   - Ⓓ she wanted to celebrate her birthday with her family

6. At the end of the story, the Beast said that he had been enchanted by _____.
   - Ⓐ an evil fairy
   - Ⓑ an old sorcerer
   - Ⓒ a wicked goblin
   - Ⓓ a cruel magician

Is It True?

Write a **T** in front of each statement that is true.
Write an **F** in front of each statement that is false.

_____ Sebastian was displeased with Brinna and Flona because they were greedy.

_____ Sebastian was thankful for the good meal and warm bed he found at the castle.

_____ The Beast was angry with Sebastian because he stole a gold plate.

_____ Beauty was very sad when Sebastian left her with the Beast.

_____ Beauty was frightened of the Beast because he treated her badly.

_____ When Sebastian fell ill, Brinna and Flona gladly took care of him.

_____ Brinna and Flona wanted Beauty to stay with them because they loved her so much.

_____ The Beast tried hard to make Beauty happy.

_____ When Beauty learned that the Beast was ill, she blamed herself.

_____ Sebastian thought that Beauty should return to the Beast in order to help him.

Underline the sentence that best describes the moral, or lesson, of this story.

Think carefully before making a decision.

Don't judge people by their appearance.

It is better to be safe than sorry.

Mind your own business.

Choose the Right Meaning

Find these highlighted words in the story. Read the sentence in which each word is found. Choose the correct meaning.

1. The word **wealthy** means _____.
   - (A) poor
   - (B) lazy
   - (C) rich
   - (D) tired

2. The word **folly** means _____.
   - (A) wisdom
   - (B) foolishness
   - (C) good sense
   - (D) thoughtfulness

3. The word **extravagant** means _____.
   - (A) ragged
   - (B) simple
   - (C) dirty
   - (D) excessive

4. The word **fragrant** means _____.
   - (A) good-tasting
   - (B) good-looking
   - (C) good-smelling
   - (D) pleasant sounding

5. The word **piteously** means _____.
   - (A) anxiously
   - (B) sorrowfully
   - (C) merrily
   - (D) gladly

6. The word **rumpled** means _____.
   - (A) hot
   - (B) green
   - (C) smooth
   - (D) wrinkled

7. The word **agony** means _____.
   - (A) restful sleep
   - (B) pain and misery
   - (C) joy and rejoicing
   - (D) noisy celebration

8. The word **vigor** means _____.
   - (A) intelligence
   - (B) weakness
   - (C) strength
   - (D) vision

9. The word **beckoned** means _____.
   - (A) called or signaled to
   - (B) slapped or punched
   - (C) disappeared
   - (D) poisoned

10. The word **morsel** means _____.
    - (A) a specially prepared dish
    - (B) a large helping of food
    - (C) a small bite of food
    - (D) leftovers

Draw and Write

Draw a picture to illustrate the meaning of each word. Look back at the story to help you.

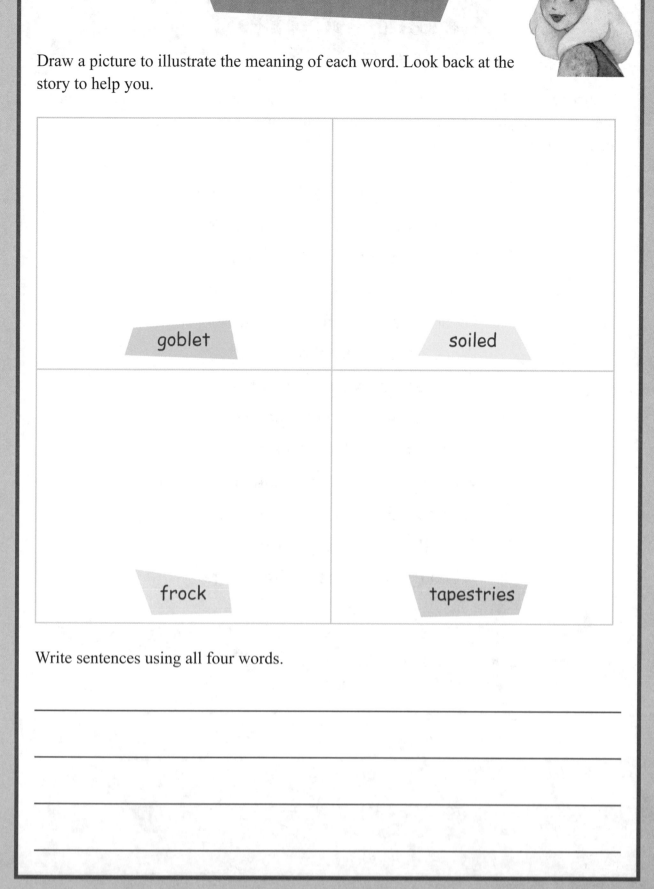

goblet

soiled

frock

tapestries

Write sentences using all four words.

_____

_____

_____

_____

Fluency: Reading with Phrasing

Practice reading the poem three times. Be sure to use a questioning voice. Notice that some of the sentences in the poem are divided into two lines. Use natural phrasing as you read these sentences.

Beauty Is

What do we know about beauty?

How do we know what it means?

Can beauty be measured by actions

Or only by that which is seen?

What do we know about beauty?

Can it only be viewed with the eyes?

Or does beauty sometimes lie hidden,

A secret behind a disguise?

What do we know about beauty?

Is it found just in nature and art?

Or is there a beauty more precious,

A beauty that lives in the heart?

Explain what the word **beauty** means to you.

_____

_____

_____

What Belongs?

List three items that belong in each category.

Things You Need to Set the Table

_____

_____

_____

Seasons of the Year

_____

_____

_____

Kinds of Jewelry

_____

_____

_____

Kinds of Flowers

_____

_____

_____

Things That Grow in a Garden

_____

_____

_____

Things That Give Light

_____

_____

_____

Members of a Family

_____

_____

_____

Tracking Tornadoes

A **tornado** is the Earth's wildest and most powerful weather event. A tornado can rip a huge tree right out of the ground. It can fling a car through the air as easily as you could toss a plastic toy. It can turn a large house into a pile of **splinters**.

The most deadly tornado in U.S. history took place in 1925. This tornado ripped through the states of Missouri, Illinois, and Indiana. It is known as the Tri-State Tornado. This tornado killed over 600 people.

Photo: N.O.A.A.

It traveled for over 200 miles. It destroyed thousands of homes and other buildings.

More recently, a powerful tornado in 1997 crushed the tiny town of Jarrell, Texas. It smashed over fifty homes and killed about 30 people!

It is easy to see why most people find tornadoes terrifying! But to many people, tornadoes are also **fascinating**. Weather scientists still do not understand exactly how and why tornadoes form. Some of these scientists actually go looking for tornadoes in order to learn more about them.

Photo: N.O.A.A.

These scientists know that the flat **prairie** country east of the Rocky Mountains is a good place to find tornadoes. This area includes the states of Texas, Oklahoma, Kansas, and Nebraska. It is often called "Tornado Alley" because so many tornadoes occur here.

People who live in this part of the country must be prepared to deal with these frightening storms. Many homes have underground basements or storm cellars where families can go in case of a tornado. This is the safest place to be during a tornado. Many towns have warning **sirens** that sound an alarm when tornadoes threaten.

Why are there so many tornadoes in Tornado Alley? On the wide Midwestern plains, several air currents collide. Cold Arctic air moves down from Canada. Warm, moist air moves up from the Gulf of Mexico. Hot, dry air flows in from the Southwestern deserts.

This **collision** of warm and cool air creates many thunderstorms. Most of these thunderstorms occur in the spring and early summer. Sometimes, a thunderstorm becomes very large. This kind of thunderstorm is called a "supercell."

It is within a supercell that a tornado is formed. Rising and falling streams of air within the storm create spinning air currents. Sometimes, these swirling winds become very strong. In a few cases, the swirling winds form a funnel cloud. More rarely, this rapidly spinning funnel cloud touches the ground. Then it becomes a tornado.

Tornado Alley

Photo: N.O.A.A.

Photo: N.O.A.A.

Chasing *Storms*

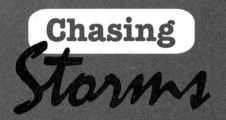

Some people who chase tornadoes are not interested in learning. They simply like the excitement of seeing a powerful storm. These people are **amateurs** *who do not have the training and information they need to be safe. They often do foolish things that put themselves and others in danger.*

They stop their cars in the middle of the road, blocking traffic. They get in the way of law enforcement or rescue efforts. They put themselves at risk of being struck by lightning. They sometimes drive **recklessly**, *especially in the difficult weather conditions created by the storms.*

Amateur storm chasers often get in the way of scientists trying to gather information. Only people with knowledge and experience should attempt to track a tornado!

Photo: Martin Lisius, courtesy Tempest Tours, Inc.

In order to study tornadoes, scientists must get close to these monster storms. They follow thunderstorms that might produce tornadoes. They drive many miles, hoping to spot a tornado as it is forming.

They use special vans and trucks. These trucks have **instruments** for recording information about the weather. They measure wind speed, **humidity**, and wind direction.

Sometimes, scientists send weather balloons into the storms. These balloons also carry instruments. They can measure temperature and wind speed inside the storms. And special airplanes fly near the storms. They use radar to study what is happening inside.

For a few years, the tornado trackers tried another **method**. They would race to get ahead of a tornado. Then, they would place a heavy package of weather instruments in the tornado's path. The trackers called this package a "Totable Tornado **Observatory**." They nicknamed it "TOTO," after the little dog in *The Wizard of Oz*. Some important information was obtained from the instruments in TOTO. For example, the wind speed in one tornado reached 280 miles per hour!

However, the scientists also learned that trying to outrun the tornado was too dangerous. Once, they watched in horror as the twisting wall of a tornado tore through a field right in front of their van. They were very lucky. No one was hurt. But they realized that the information they might gain was not worth risking their lives. Somewhat sadly, they put TOTO into **storage**.

The scientists who study tornadoes are willing to face great danger. They want to learn why tornadoes develop in some thunderstorms but not in others. They want to be able to predict the formation of tornadoes. This would make it possible to warn people that a tornado is coming. Earlier warnings could help save lives.

Each year, about 1,000 tornadoes touch down in the United States. Most last only a short time. Most do little or no harm. But a few are terrible. Scientists do not think that anything can be done to prevent tornadoes. But they hope that their work will lead to new understanding of these **dramatic** and deadly storms.

Photo: N.O.A.A.

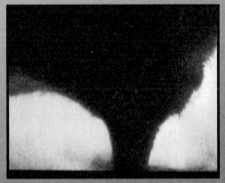

Photo: N.O.A.A.

Amazing Stories

As the tornado spins, it pulls up dust and dirt. Sometimes it picks up heavier objects. In one case, a tornado picked up a school bus and then dropped it in the school's auditorium.

Another tornado lifted a passenger train from the tracks and tossed it 80 feet. Nearly 200 people were onboard the train. Although many were injured, only one person was killed.

There are amazing stories about tornadoes picking up animals and even people, and setting them down at great distances, unhurt. Some of these accounts may be tall tales, but others are well documented. For example, in April 1974 an F5 tornado leveled a farmhouse in Xenia, Ohio. Left unharmed, however, were three fragile items: a mirror, a case of eggs, and a box of Christmas ornaments.

Questions About
Tracking Tornadoes

Photo: N.O.A.A.

Fill in the circle that best answers each question.

1. In which of these states is a tornado most likely to occur?
   - Ⓐ Maine
   - Ⓑ Hawaii
   - Ⓒ New York
   - Ⓓ Oklahoma

2. The collision of warm and cool air currents often creates _____.
   - Ⓐ a thunderstorm
   - Ⓑ a snowstorm
   - Ⓒ a frosty day
   - Ⓓ a clear sky

3. The swirling winds of a tornado are shaped like _____.
   - Ⓐ an hourglass
   - Ⓑ a funnel
   - Ⓒ a spoon
   - Ⓓ a tree

4. Scientists study tornadoes because they hope to _____.
   - Ⓐ predict when tornadoes will occur
   - Ⓑ watch tornadoes destroy houses
   - Ⓒ have fun in the rain
   - Ⓓ see a hailstorm

5. A strong thunderstorm in which a tornado forms is called _____.
   - Ⓐ a powercloud
   - Ⓑ a giantsize
   - Ⓒ a supercell
   - Ⓓ a rainbow

6. Which of the following do scientists use to gather information about storms?
   - Ⓐ a helicopter
   - Ⓑ a parachute
   - Ⓒ a rocket
   - Ⓓ a weather balloon

Write About the Story

1. Why do people find tornadoes terrifying?

_____

_____

2. Where is the safest place to be during a tornado?

_____

_____

3. What was the purpose of TOTO?

_____

_____

4. Why did scientists decide to stop using TOTO?

_____

_____

5. Give three reasons why amateur storm chasers sometimes cause problems.

_____

_____

_____

6. Would you like to see a tornado? Why or why not?

_____

_____

Choose the Right Meaning

Find these highlighted words in the story. Read the sentence in which each word is found. Choose the correct meaning.

1. A **siren** is _____.
   - Ⓐ a loud alarm or danger signal
   - Ⓑ a printed announcement
   - Ⓒ a newspaper
   - Ⓓ a clock

2. **Humidity** is the _____.
   - Ⓐ speed of the wind
   - Ⓑ temperature at ground level
   - Ⓒ amount of moisture in the air
   - Ⓓ amount of snowfall in a given year

3. Which of the following is a kind of **instrument**?
   - Ⓐ a scientist
   - Ⓑ a tornado
   - Ⓒ a state
   - Ⓓ a thermometer

4. The word **recklessly** means about the same as _____.
   - Ⓐ carefully
   - Ⓑ carelessly
   - Ⓒ cautiously
   - Ⓓ thoughtfully

5. In this story, the word **storage** means _____.
   - Ⓐ a place to keep things that are not in use
   - Ⓑ a place to bury things
   - Ⓒ a place to buy things
   - Ⓓ a place to live

6. A **dramatic** event is one that is _____.
   - Ⓐ funny and comical
   - Ⓑ dull and uninteresting
   - Ⓒ common and ordinary
   - Ⓓ spectacular and theatrical

7. Which of the following is an antonym for **amateurs**?
   - Ⓐ beginners
   - Ⓑ novices
   - Ⓒ professionals
   - Ⓓ trainees

8. Which of the following is <u>not</u> a meaning for **method**?
   - Ⓐ rule
   - Ⓑ process
   - Ⓒ technique
   - Ⓓ procedure

9. Something that is **fascinating** is _____.
   - Ⓐ boring
   - Ⓑ bright
   - Ⓒ difficult
   - Ⓓ interesting

10. An **observatory** is used to _____.
    - Ⓐ cook things
    - Ⓑ study things
    - Ⓒ store things
    - Ⓓ paint things

Draw and Write

Draw a picture to illustrate the meaning of each word. Look back at the story to help you.

splinters	prairie
collision	tornado

Write sentences using all four words.

_____

_____

_____

Fact or Opinion?

A fact tells information that is true.
An opinion tells about someone's thoughts or feelings.

Write **fact** or **opinion** after each statement.

1. Tornadoes are very powerful storms. _____

2. Tornadoes form within supercells. _____

3. It would be fun to be a tornado tracker. _____

4. People should not live in places where tornadoes occur. _____

5. Scientists who study tornadoes are foolish. _____

6. Tornadoes are exciting and interesting. _____

7. Most tornadoes take place in spring and early summer. _____

8. A storm cellar is a good place to go during a tornado. _____

Write two or three sentences telling how you might feel and what you might do if you saw a tornado approaching your house.

_____

_____

_____

_____

_____

Graphing Tornadoes

Use the information in the graph to answer the questions that follow.

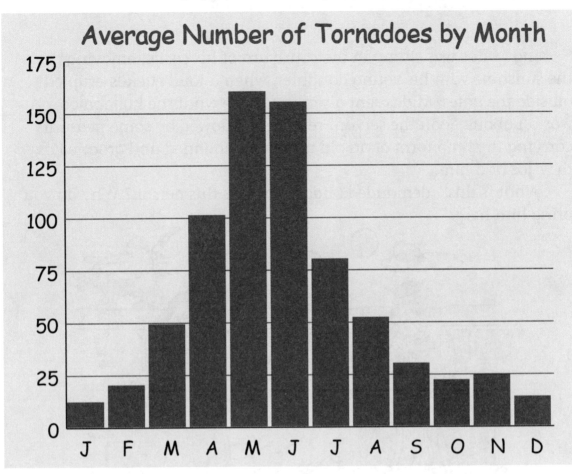

Average Number of Tornadoes by Month

1. In which month do the greatest number of tornadoes usually occur?

_____

2. In which month are tornadoes least likely to occur?

_____

3. What is the average number of tornadoes in November?

_____

4. What is the average number of tornadoes in the month you were born?

_____

THE MIDAS TOUCH

A GREEK MYTH

King Midas was sitting in the courtyard of his castle, enjoying the sunshine with his young daughter, when a loud **ruckus** erupted outside the gates. Midas sent a servant to see what the **hullabaloo** was all about. Soon the servant returned, followed by some peasants carrying the limp form of an old man, who moaned and groaned as they **jostled** him.

"What is this!" demanded Midas. "Who is this person? Why do you bring him here?"

"Sire," answered the servant, "this is an old man. He says his name is Silenus. He is unwell. He is in need of a place to rest and **recover**."

"Very well," said Midas. "Find him a bed and a nurse. We will do all we can for him."

Gradually, Silenus recovered. Midas treated him with kindness and shared all the hospitality the castle had to offer. After a week had passed, a knock came at the castle gate. Bacchus, the god of the vineyards, **strode** into the courtyard.

Reading • EMC 4533 • ©2005 by Evan-Moor Corp.

"Greetings," stammered Midas in surprise. "How may I serve you?"

Bacchus laughed and answered, "You have it all wrong, Midas. I have come to serve you!"

"But why?" asked Midas in surprise. "Why should a god serve a **mere** king?"

"Because you have done me a great kindness," answered Bacchus. "You see, Silenus is my old schoolmaster. I am very fond of him. I am grateful for all you have done for him, and I wish to repay you. Come, Midas, name your reward. Make any wish you like, and I shall fulfill it."

Now Midas, though a kind man, was overly fond of wealth, and the **opportunity** that lay before him seemed too good to be true. With his heart thumping in his throat, Midas made his wish. "I wish that whatever I touch shall turn into gold, from this moment forward!"

Bacchus looked thoughtful. "Are you sure that is wise, Midas?" he asked. "Are you certain that is what you want?"

"Oh, yes," breathed Midas. "I can imagine no greater gift."

"Very well," said Bacchus, in a **doubtful** tone. "It is done. Now, let my servants fetch Silenus, and we shall be away."

As soon as Bacchus had swept out the gate, King Midas rushed to test his new powers. He reached for his walking stick and was amazed to see it change to shining gold as he lifted it. He picked up a small pebble from the garden path and watched as it was instantly **transformed** into a **nugget** of purest gold. He plucked a flower from a nearby bush. In his hand, it became a stem of **precious** metal.

Excited, he ran into the castle, calling for his servants. "We must celebrate!" he exclaimed. "Fetch my family and all the nobles of the town. Set the table for a great feast. I am the wealthiest man in the world!"

Laughing softly to himself, King Midas strode up and down the paths in his courtyard while the servants rushed about to do his bidding. Soon, all was ready for the festivities. King Midas welcomed family and friends to his home and **ushered** them all to the table in the great hall. Everyone sat down and began to eat with pleasure.

King Midas watched for a moment, filled with joy. Then he picked up a roll and hungrily took a bite.

"What's this?" yelped Midas, as his teeth met the hard surface and bounced off. Naturally, he could not eat the bread, for it had turned to gold. He lifted his goblet to take a sip of wine, but the goblet and the liquid it held had turned to **solid** gold.

All the people gathered at the table looked at him in amazement. They began to buzz excitedly among themselves. Never had they seen such miraculous events. But Midas now realized that he had been very foolish indeed. He dropped his head upon the table and began to weep. His little daughter, taking pity, ran to his side. In his grief, Midas embraced her, whereupon she immediately froze into a perfect golden **replica** of a little girl. Midas drew back in horror at the sight of his dear daughter standing like a **brilliant** statue.

"What have I done?" he wailed. "Oh, curse my selfishness! Bacchus, please take away this **cruel** gift," he begged. "I regret my greed and my folly. Please have **mercy** on me, and take away this hateful gift."

Suddenly, Midas heard the voice of Bacchus echoing down the long hall. "Very well," said the voice. "Go now and bathe yourself in the river Pactolus. Go forth to the very place where this river springs from the Earth and wash yourself in its waters. Take your daughter and bathe her, too."

Midas grabbed up his daughter and rushed out into the hills. He did exactly as Bacchus had told him. He bathed himself in the spring, then **plunged** his daughter into the waters. Immediately, she was restored from cold metal to rosy flesh. At the same moment, the waters of the river became as golden as a field of ripe grain.

Laughing with joy, Midas grabbed the nearest object, a small buttercup growing near the stream. It did not turn to gold, but retained its soft and lovely petals as he tucked it into his daughter's curls.

"Hooray!" shouted Midas. "I have never been so happy in my life."

Midas took his daughter's hand, and together they walked back across the hills and meadows to the castle.

To this day, those who walk beside the Pactolus River will see a golden river flowing over golden sandy banks, a reminder of King Midas and his terrible golden touch.

Questions About
THE MIDAS TOUCH

Fill in the circle that best answers each question.

1. Why did the peasants bring the old man to King Midas?
   - Ⓐ The old man was sick and needed help.
   - Ⓑ The old man and King Midas were friends.
   - Ⓒ The old man wanted to borrow some money.
   - Ⓓ The old man wanted to sell King Midas a pair of shoes.

2. Why did Bacchus want to give Midas a gift?
   - Ⓐ He felt sorry for Midas.
   - Ⓑ Midas was in the hospital.
   - Ⓒ He wanted Midas to be his friend.
   - Ⓓ He was grateful to Midas for his kindness to the old schoolmaster.

3. Why did Midas plan a celebration?
   - Ⓐ It was his birthday.
   - Ⓑ It was his daughter's birthday.
   - Ⓒ He was excited about his newfound wealth.
   - Ⓓ He was happy that Silenus had recovered his health.

4. Why did Midas start to cry during the feast?
   - Ⓐ He realized that the golden touch was really a curse.
   - Ⓑ He had a headache.
   - Ⓒ He was very happy.
   - Ⓓ He felt lonely.

5. When Midas realized what he had done, he felt ashamed of his _____.
   - Ⓐ wealth
   - Ⓑ greed
   - Ⓒ cruelty
   - Ⓓ unkindness

6. What do you think this story is saying?
   - Ⓐ Think before you ask for something.
   - Ⓑ Don't accept a reward for helping people.
   - Ⓒ Flowers are more precious than gold.
   - Ⓓ Riches alone will not make you happy.

Put It in Order

In the story, Midas experiences several different emotions. Number them in the order in which they take place in the story.

_____ Midas felt **relieved** and **happy** when he washed away his golden touch.

_____ Midas felt **annoyed** when Silenus was brought into the courtyard.

_____ Midas felt **joyful** as he prepared for the feast.

_____ Midas felt **confused** when Bacchus came to visit him.

_____ Midas felt **excited** when Bacchus offered him a reward.

_____ Midas felt **miserable** when he turned his daughter into gold.

_____ Midas felt **surprised** when he tried to bite into a piece of bread.

Choose one of the emotions mentioned above. Write about a time when you have experienced this emotion.

_____

_____

_____

_____

Choose the Right Meaning

Find these highlighted words in the story. Read the sentence in which each word is found. Choose the correct meaning.

1. The word **jostled** means _____.
   - Ⓐ played a game
   - Ⓑ tripped and fell
   - Ⓒ sat straight and tall
   - Ⓓ bumped and pushed

2. The word **nugget** means _____.
   - Ⓐ a small lump
   - Ⓑ a plank
   - Ⓒ a book
   - Ⓓ a frog

3. The word **recover** means _____.
   - Ⓐ to get smaller
   - Ⓑ to get bigger
   - Ⓒ to get better
   - Ⓓ to be sad

4. The word **replica** means _____.
   - Ⓐ a beautiful flower
   - Ⓑ an exact copy
   - Ⓒ a wool coat
   - Ⓓ an old book

5. The word **plunged** means _____.
   - Ⓐ leaped or flew over
   - Ⓑ jumped or dived in
   - Ⓒ read carefully
   - Ⓓ took a nap

6. The word **transformed** means _____.
   - Ⓐ explained
   - Ⓑ smashed
   - Ⓒ changed
   - Ⓓ painted

7. The word **doubtful** means _____.
   - Ⓐ uncertain
   - Ⓑ unkind
   - Ⓒ unhappy
   - Ⓓ unfeeling

8. The word **mercy** means _____.
   - Ⓐ cruel laughter
   - Ⓑ revenge and anger
   - Ⓒ misery and sadness
   - Ⓓ kindness and pity

9. The word **ruckus** means _____.
   - Ⓐ celebration
   - Ⓑ commotion
   - Ⓒ backpack
   - Ⓓ ball game

10. The word **opportunity** means _____.
   - Ⓐ chance
   - Ⓑ job
   - Ⓒ time
   - Ⓓ permission

Reading • EMC 4533 • ©2005 by Evan-Moor Corp.

Which Word Fits?

Complete each sentence using a word from the box. If you need help with the meaning of the words, look for them in the story and read the sentences in which they are found.

hullabaloo	mere	precious	ushered
strode	solid	cruel	brilliant

1. In the bitter cold weather, the river froze _____.

2. The _____ sunlight sparkled on the water.

3. The actor _____ to the center of the stage with great confidence.

4. Mr. Keenan _____ his clients into the conference room.

5. Jane thought that her mom was _____ because she would not let her have a kitten.

6. Bradley finished the difficult test in a _____ fifteen minutes.

7. A _____ erupted at the zoo when the gorillas escaped from their cages.

8. Grandmother's antique ring is set with _____ stones.

More and Most

Read these rules:

- We add the suffixes –er and –est to adjectives to compare size or amount.

  great   great**er** = more great   great**est** = most great

- When a word ends in y, change the y to i and then add er or est.

  wealthy   wealth**ier** = more wealthy   wealth**iest** = most wealthy

- When a word ends in e, drop the e and add er or est.

  litt**le**   litt**ler** = more little   litt**lest** = most little

Add er and est to each word.

Adjective	More	Most
lovely	_____	_____
shiny	_____	_____
rich	_____	_____
tiny	_____	_____
greedy	_____	_____
old	_____	_____
kind	_____	_____
rough	_____	_____
bright	_____	_____
simple	_____	_____
gentle	_____	_____
pure	_____	_____

       Reading • EMC 4533 • ©2005 by Evan-Moor Corp.

Understanding Similes

Similes compare two things using the words like or as.

The boy was as *strong as an ox.*

The calm lake was like *a mirror.*

These similes are found in "The Midas Touch":

Midas drew back in horror at the sight of his dear daughter standing like a statue.

At the same moment, the waters of the river became as golden as a field of ripe grain.

Complete each sentence with a simile of your own.

1. The sleeping baby was as quiet as _____.

2. Her eyes were shining like _____.

3. The frozen ground was as hard as _____.

4. Our puppy is as gentle as _____.

5. Jim is as tall as _____.

6. The full moon was like _____.

7. The rain was falling like _____.

8. My happy heart felt as light as _____.

Otzi the Iceman

igh in a beautiful Alpine valley on the border of Italy and Austria, a young couple went out for a hike. It was a lovely autumn afternoon in 1991. As the hikers made their way across the snow-covered rocks, they made a chilling discovery. Poking out from the melting ice was a human skull!

Looking closer, the **hikers** found that an entire body lay buried in the ice. They quickly left the scene and called the police.

Police **investigators** came to look at the body. They dug at the ice and tried to free the body. They were not able to pry it loose. Their efforts damaged the body and the scraps of clothing it was wearing. The police decided to get some help.

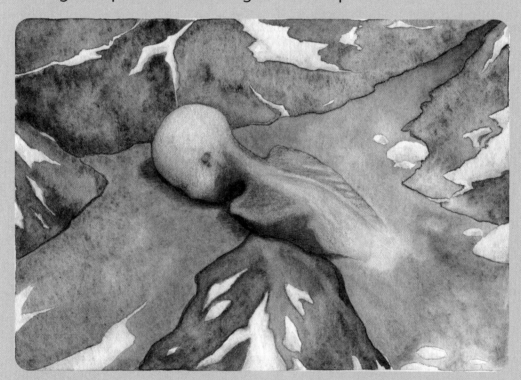

The police called in a **scientist** to look at the iceman. The scientist noticed that the iceman's body looked like a mummy. He knew it was very old. He realized that this was a very important discovery. He dug the iceman's body out of the ice as carefully as he could. The iceman was then flown to a **laboratory**.

In the lab, an **archaeologist** examined the body. He also looked at the tools and other items that had been found nearby. These included an ax with a wooden handle and a copper blade, a small stone knife, and a large bow with a quiver of arrows. The study of these items showed that they were over 5,000 years old!

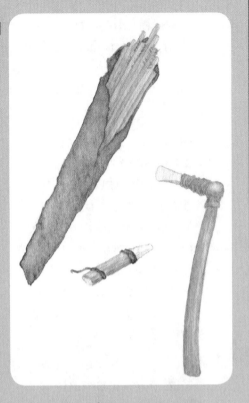

The people who lived in the region were very excited by this news. They gave the iceman a name. They called him Otzi because he had been found near the Otztal valley. As news of the iceman spread, people all around the world took an interest. Who was Otzi the Iceman? Where did he come from? How did he live? Why did he die?

Scientists have come a long way toward answering these questions. They have learned a great deal from Otzi's belongings about what life was like 5,000 years ago. They know that Otzi's clothing was made from animal skins. His shoes were made of the skins of bear, deer, and wild goat. These shoes were stuffed with

dried grass to make them warmer. He also had a shirt and pants made of skins. He wore a cap made of fur. He had a cape made of braided grasses. He carried a backpack and some small pouches made of birch bark.

In addition to his weapons, he had some tools. He had a tool for sharpening flint so that he could make arrowheads. He had an **awl** and some string for repairing his shoes and clothing. And he had a kit for starting fires.

He also had a slice of meat, some berries, and some mushrooms. Certainly, Otzi and the other people of his time knew how to hunt and gather food. It was clear they had to make their own clothing, as well as their own tools and weapons.

The only item that Otzi had not made for himself was probably his fine copper ax. It would have required special skills and special tools to make such an ax. Otzi probably obtained the ax from a **coppersmith**. It was most likely a highly prized possession.

This drawing shows how Otzi may have looked.

Scientists have also learned a lot from studying Otzi's body. They believe that he had a diet made up largely of grains. In Otzi's time, grains were ground between rocks. Tiny bits of rock became mixed into the grain. As people ate the grain, the rock **particles** ground away at their teeth. Otzi's teeth showed signs of this kind of wear. When they examined the **contents** of Otzi's stomach, they found traces of meat along with two kinds of grain.

By examining the **minerals** in his teeth and bones, they have learned that Otzi spent his entire life in the mountain valleys near the place where his body was found. They believe that he was born in a small village near present-day Bolzano, Italy, and that he probably did not travel more than 40 miles from that spot throughout his life.

Perhaps most startling is the discovery of how Otzi died. Scientists made X-rays of Otzi's body. They found that Otzi had been in a fight in the hours before he died. In fact, a stone arrowhead remains embedded inside Otzi's shoulder. He has a severe cut across his right hand. Scientists are still studying the body to determine if there are other injuries as well.

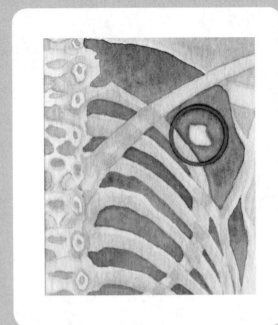

No one knows for sure who attacked Otzi. **Researchers** believe, however, that he escaped his **attackers** before he died. They believe that Otzi was able to flee up the mountain and hide. This is because Otzi's tools and weapons—even his splendid ax—were at his side when he died. If the attackers had found him, they would surely have taken these **valuable** objects.

Instead, scientists believe that Otzi found a place to rest. He placed all his belongings neatly at his side, and stretched out on the ground. He was weak from loss of blood and in great pain from his injuries. Otzi struggled to stay alive, but his wounds were too **severe**. After some hours had passed, Otzi died. Snow fell, covering his body and leaving no trace of his passing.

For thousands of years, snow fell on the mountain. Otzi became buried deeper and deeper inside the heart of the glacier. There he remained until the melting ice revealed him to the hikers.

Today, Otzi rests inside a specially built, ice-lined case in the South Tyrol Museum of Archaeology in Bolzano, Italy. This museum is not far from where Otzi was born, and where he lived out his life. **Tourists** flock to the museum to gaze at Otzi in wonder. Scientists continue to study Otzi for more clues about his life and death. And archaeologists are searching the area where Otzi's body was discovered to see if more bodies or **artifacts** can be found in the melting ice.

Otzi the Iceman is the oldest human body ever found. Because of Otzi, we can touch the distant past. We can imagine the lives of our human ancestors. Because of Otzi, we can look back through time and glimpse an ancient world.

Reading • EMC 4533 • ©2005 by Evan-Moor Corp.

Questions About
Otzi the Iceman

Fill in the circle that best answers each question.

1. How was Otzi found?
   - Ⓐ A camper's dog dug him up.
   - Ⓑ He washed up on the shore of a lake.
   - Ⓒ Hikers saw his skull sticking out of the ice.
   - Ⓓ He was uncovered by a landslide.

2. Why was this discovery called "the Iceman"?
   - Ⓐ The body was very cold.
   - Ⓑ The body had been buried in ice.
   - Ⓒ He lived during the Ice Age.
   - Ⓓ He had to be refrigerated to preserve him.

3. Scientists believe Otzi lived about _____.
   - Ⓐ 500 years ago
   - Ⓑ 1,000 years ago
   - Ⓒ 2,000 years ago
   - Ⓓ 5,000 years ago

4. Otzi probably died of injuries he received _____.
   - Ⓐ in a fall
   - Ⓑ in a fight
   - Ⓒ from a bear
   - Ⓓ while making a fire

5. No one found Otzi for many years because has was _____.
   - Ⓐ covered with sand
   - Ⓑ hidden in deep woods
   - Ⓒ buried in the snow and ice
   - Ⓓ at the bottom a deep lake

6. Which of these statements about Otzi is true?
   - Ⓐ Otzi is the oldest human body ever found.
   - Ⓑ Otzi was found in Germany.
   - Ⓒ Otzi was female.
   - Ⓓ Otzi had a gun.

Write About the Story

1. The article said that Otzi was found in the autumn. How is the time of year important to the discovery?

_____

_____

_____

2. How was Otzi's body preserved for so many years?

_____

_____

3. Why were Otzi's teeth worn away?

_____

_____

4. What do scientists hope to learn by studying Otzi and his belongings?

_____

_____

5. Would you like to see Otzi? Why or why not?

_____

_____

_____

Reading • EMC 4533 • ©2005 by Evan-Moor Corp.

Choose the Right Meaning

Find these highlighted words in the story. Read the sentence in which each word is found. Choose the correct meaning.

1. A **hiker** is a person who _____.
   - Ⓐ plays a musical instrument
   - Ⓑ takes long walks
   - Ⓒ paddles a boat
   - Ⓓ sings a song

2. An **archaeologist** is a person who _____.
   - Ⓐ studies old objects to learn about the past
   - Ⓑ studies new technology
   - Ⓒ repairs broken pottery
   - Ⓓ designs buildings

3. A **tourist** is a person who likes to _____.
   - Ⓐ tell stories
   - Ⓑ ride buses
   - Ⓒ stay at home
   - Ⓓ go sightseeing

4. A **scientist** is a person who _____.
   - Ⓐ investigates to learn new facts
   - Ⓑ likes to watch action movies
   - Ⓒ writes in a journal
   - Ⓓ reads old books

5. A police **investigator** is a person who _____.
   - Ⓐ flies an airplane
   - Ⓑ repairs telephone lines
   - Ⓒ looks for clues about crimes
   - Ⓓ cooks meals in fine restaurants

6. An **attacker** is a person who _____.
   - Ⓐ uses force to harm
   - Ⓑ follows someone
   - Ⓒ sneaks around
   - Ⓓ hides in bushes

7. A **coppersmith** is a person who _____.
   - Ⓐ makes guns
   - Ⓑ builds barns
   - Ⓒ makes barrels
   - Ⓓ makes metal items

8. A **researcher** is a person who _____.
   - Ⓐ looks for lost people
   - Ⓑ tries to discover facts
   - Ⓒ assists in an operating room
   - Ⓓ navigates a sailing ship

Which Word Fits?

Complete each sentence using a word from the box. If you need
help with the meaning of the words, look for them in the story
and read the sentences in which they are found.

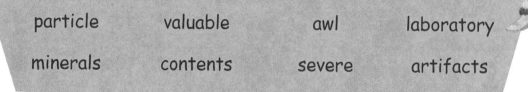

| particle | valuable | awl | laboratory |
| minerals | contents | severe | artifacts |

1. An _____ is a tool for punching holes through leather.

2. We saw a display of ancient _____ in the museum.

3. Vegetables are important sources of vitamins and _____ .

4. This bracelet is very _____ to me because my grandmother
gave it to me.

5. A _____ is a tiny, little piece of something.

6. Maggie looked through the _____ of her backpack to
find a pencil.

7. During the _____ thunderstorm, the lights went out
for two hours.

8. The researchers did some experiments in the _____ .

In the Dictionary

Place the words from the word box in order on the correct dictionary page below.

awl	severe	valley	artifact	string	ancient
very	discover	weapon	determine	weak	splendid
museum	ancestor	mummy	stomach	injury	wooden
item	scene	wound	mineral	mountain	scientist

alpine │ escape

1. _____
2. _____
3. _____
4. _____
5. _____
6. _____

sandstone │ study

1. _____
2. _____
3. _____
4. _____
5. _____
6. _____

ice │ mushroom

1. _____
2. _____
3. _____
4. _____
5. _____
6. _____

tools │ wound

1. _____
2. _____
3. _____
4. _____
5. _____
6. _____

Adding -ing

The suffix -ing is added to a verb to show action that is ongoing.

When the verb ends in e, you drop the e and add ing.

For example: leave   leaving

Add the suffix **-ing** to each word below.

1. chill   _____

2. poke   _____

3. melt   _____

4. examine   _____

5. look   _____

6. wear   _____

7. answer   _____

8. startle   _____

9. sharpen   _____

10. study   _____

11. pass   _____

12. determine   _____

Write three sentences. Use an -ing word from the list above in each sentence.

_____

_____

_____

THE TIGER AND THE JACKALS

One day, Devak took his daughter Mita out to the woods. He planned to tell her a story that his father had told him here in these same woods not so long ago.

"My girl," Devak began, "this is a story that has been in our family for generations. It was my favorite story when I was your age. Your grandfather brought me here to tell it to me. And now I am going to tell it to you."

Mita sat quietly, eager to hear the tale. She looked around at the bright birds in the trees and at the lush, green **foliage**. She looked up at the sun through the leaves of the trees and was **entranced**. After letting her soak in the beauty of the forest, Devak began to tell the story.

Once, a long time ago in these very woods, there lived a great tiger. There were many other animals as well, but the tiger was the king of the forest. When he was hungry, he would let out a huge growl. The little animals would tremble in their tracks, frozen with fear. The tiger would then come along and **devour** them until he had eaten his fill.

Life was good for the tiger. He lived in this beautiful forest, had all the food he could want, and he didn't even have to work in order to catch it. He just spent his days **lolling** about in the shade. But one day, things changed. The tiger got hungry and let out a mighty roar. Strangely, the animals he expected to see **cowering** on the ground were nowhere to be found.

After a few moments of utter confusion, it slowly dawned on the tiger that he had been far too greedy. He had failed to consider that in his pursuit of comfort and pleasure, he had steadily been eating the forest out of **inhabitants**. In fact, he became aware that he was now alone in the forest. He had only the birds in the trees to keep him company.

The tiger sat down to think about his new and troubling situation. He was filled with gloom. As he sat feeling sorry for himself and regretting his gluttonous ways, he caught a flash of movement among the leaves. Behind a nearby bush, he spotted a pair of small **mangy** jackals. Suddenly, he forgot all about being too greedy.

Instead, his hunger overwhelmed his feelings of guilt. He let out a mighty roar, expecting the jackals to fall on the ground in terror. But unlike the animals in the past, the jackals did not just stand there trembling. Instead, they began to run.

Reading • EMC 4533 • ©2005 by Evan-Moor Corp.

This was a shock to the tiger. It had been years since he had been forced to **pursue** his prey, but he did so now. He chased behind the jackals, growling and snarling every step of the way.

The jackals could see that the tiger was gaining on them. The smaller of the two **scrawny** creatures spoke. "I fear he is going to catch us."

But the larger jackal responded, "Oh no, don't worry about that. Just do as I tell you."

In the blink of an eye, the jackals **bolted** into some thick bushes. Just as quickly, they came bounding out from where they had just gone in. Now they were heading directly toward the tiger! As they approached the beast, they both looked terrified.

"That's better!" the tiger roared, laughing and full of pride. "Why did you run from me?" he asked as they came to a halt in front of him.

"Ah yes, that's a good question," said the larger jackal. "But the better question is why did we stop running from you and come to stand before you now?"

The tiger was clearly annoyed by the little **canine** and was ready to dispense with the conversation and enjoy his dinner. But his curiosity was aroused by the clever jackal's question.

"Because I am a terrifying, predatory beast, and you knew you hadn't a chance of escape," the tiger said.

"Oh no," said the jackal. "I'm afraid that is not the case. In fact, we ran in this direction because there is another tiger in these woods, much larger and more terrible than you. He is just on the other side of those bushes."

The tiger laughed, but inside he was worried. He had not left his patch of the forest for many years, and it was possible that there was indeed another tiger.

"Come with us now," said the smaller jackal, "and we'll show him to you. Perhaps one of you will kill the other, and we will have one less tiger to worry about."

The **insolence** and **brashness** of the jackals were truly amazing, and the tiger roared at the remark. But he understood the nature of a challenge, and so he followed the jackals.

Together, the three animals crashed through the underbrush until they came out into a small clearing. In the clearing, there was a hole in the ground. The jackals knew about this hole. They had watched as some strange-looking animals who stood upright on two feet dug deep into the earth. They had watched as these odd creatures took water from the hole. They themselves had crept near to examine the hole. They hoped that the tiger would not be as clever.

"The other tiger lives down in this den," said the larger jackal as they approached the hole, which, of course, was really a well. "But be careful. He is very fierce and frightening."

The tiger was wary, but he could not show fear. He marched up to the side of the well and peered over, wearing his most fearsome expression.

Sure enough, he saw a tiger looking up at him with teeth bared and eyes narrowed.

"It's true!" he exclaimed, as he looked down again and growled at the other tiger, who growled right back. The sound was frightful, and the tiger would have liked to run away that very instant. But he knew that the jackals were observing him. Not wanting **to lose face**, he realized he must challenge this new tiger that was intruding on his territory.

He turned to the jackals and snarled, "I will go down into his den and take care of this foolish tiger. I will be back for you two in a moment."

With that, the tiger bared his teeth and his claws and dove into the well toward the other tiger.

When the jackals heard the splash, they began dancing around the well in celebration. They had tricked the tiger and saved themselves. They giggled and cheered as they heard the tiger thrashing in the water. Soon, there was nothing but silence from the well.

In time, the animals came back to the forest, daughter, and you must always be careful, for even the tiger again walks these ways. And though he is no longer lazy and greedy, he may remember how he was tricked. He will not be easily fooled again.

Questions About
THE TIGER ᴬᴺᴰ THE JACKALS

Fill in the circle that best answers each question.

1. The tiger normally got his food by _____.
   - Ⓐ chasing it until he caught it
   - Ⓑ waiting for people to bring it to him
   - Ⓒ catching his prey while they were sleeping
   - Ⓓ frightening his prey so much that they could not move

2. One day, the tiger suddenly realized that _____.
   - Ⓐ he had eaten all the animals in the forest
   - Ⓑ the animals had found new homes
   - Ⓒ he missed the other animals
   - Ⓓ he had grown too fat to hunt

3. When the tiger roared at the jackals, they _____.
   - Ⓐ fell on the ground in fear
   - Ⓑ laughed at the tiger
   - Ⓒ ran away
   - Ⓓ cried

4. The jackals tricked the tiger into _____.
   - Ⓐ falling into a trap
   - Ⓑ leaping off a cliff
   - Ⓒ jumping into a well
   - Ⓓ tumbling into a pool of quicksand

5. Devak warned Mita to be careful in the forest because _____.
   - Ⓐ the little animals had come back
   - Ⓑ there could be a tiger in the forest
   - Ⓒ there could be a jackal in the forest
   - Ⓓ there could be an elephant in the forest

6. Why did Devak bring Mita into the forest to tell her this story?
   - Ⓐ Because it was too cold in the house.
   - Ⓑ Because he wanted her to help him hunt for food.
   - Ⓒ Because he hoped they would see a rabbit in the forest.
   - Ⓓ Because his father had told him the story in the forest.

Write About the Story

1. How did the tiger's feelings change when he saw the jackals in the bushes?

_____

_____

_____

2. Why did the jackals run away from the tiger at first?

_____

_____

3. Why did the jackals run back toward the tiger?

_____

_____

4. What kind of creatures dug the well?

_____

5. Why did the tiger feel he had to jump into the well?

_____

_____

6. In what way might this story change Mita's behavior?

_____

_____

Choose the Right Meaning

Find these highlighted words in the story. Read the sentence in which each word is found. Choose the correct meaning.

1. The word **lolling** means _____.
   - Ⓐ bashing brutally
   - Ⓑ lounging lazily
   - Ⓒ jumping jerkily
   - Ⓓ sitting sadly

2. The word **cowering** means _____.
   - Ⓐ calling out
   - Ⓑ cooking
   - Ⓒ cringing
   - Ⓓ crying

3. The word **mangy** means _____.
   - Ⓐ scruffy
   - Ⓑ sleek
   - Ⓒ fluffy
   - Ⓓ blue

4. The word **insolence** means _____.
   - Ⓐ rudeness
   - Ⓑ joyfulness
   - Ⓒ happiness
   - Ⓓ sleepiness

5. The word **bolted** means _____.
   - Ⓐ went to sleep
   - Ⓑ swallowed
   - Ⓒ ran away quickly
   - Ⓓ hid

6. The word **brashness** means _____.
   - Ⓐ grumpiness
   - Ⓑ boldness and foolhardiness
   - Ⓒ sweetness and gentleness
   - Ⓓ shyness and bashfulness

7. The word **entranced** means _____.
   - Ⓐ worried
   - Ⓑ excited
   - Ⓒ annoyed
   - Ⓓ spellbound

8. The word **devour** means to _____.
   - Ⓐ tie up
   - Ⓑ eat hungrily
   - Ⓒ scold angrily
   - Ⓓ sneak up on

9. The phrase **to lose face** means to _____.
   - Ⓐ hide from view
   - Ⓑ turn the other way
   - Ⓒ look undignified
   - Ⓓ cover up the face

10. The word **pursue** means to _____.
   - Ⓐ ask for help
   - Ⓑ look high and low
   - Ⓒ read carefully
   - Ⓓ chase after

Draw and Write

Draw a picture to illustrate the meaning of each word. Look back at the story to help you.

inhabitants	canine
foliage	scrawny

Write a sentence using at least one of these words.

_____

_____

Fluency: Reading Dialog with Expression

When you read with expression, you make your voice really show what the characters are feeling. You change your voice so that each character sounds different.

Practice reading this dialog from the story. It takes place when the jackals run back and sit down in front of the tiger. Then read the dialog aloud to a friend or family member. Remember to read with expression!

Tiger: "That's better! Why did you run from me?"

Bigger Jackal: "Ah yes, that's a good question. But the better question is why did we stop running from you and come to stand before you now?"

Tiger: "Because I am a terrifying predatory beast, and you knew you hadn't a chance of escape!"

Bigger Jackal: "Oh no, I'm afraid that is not the case. In fact, we ran in this direction because there is another tiger in these woods, much larger and more terrible than you. He is just on the other side of those bushes."

Tiger: "Ha, ha, ha. That is not true!"

Smaller Jackal: "Come with us now, and we'll show him to you. Perhaps one of you will kill the other, and we will have one less tiger to worry about."

Reading • EMC 4533 • ©2005 by Evan-Moor Corp.

What Do You Think?

Describe your favorite part of the story.

_____

_____

_____

Why did you like this part of the story best?

_____

_____

Draw a picture to illustrate this part of the story.

Silkworms

When you think of a farm, you probably think of animals such as cows, pigs, horses, and sheep. But did you know that some farmers raise caterpillars? It's true! Silk farmers raise millions and millions of caterpillars each year. These caterpillars are often called "silkworms," even though they are not worms at all.

Farmers raise silkworms to obtain the special fibers they produce. These fibers are used to make silk, one of the strongest, lightest, and most beautiful **fabrics** known to humans. It seems incredible that such lovely material is made by caterpillars!

To understand how silkworms make this amazing fiber, we have to look at the silkworm's life cycle.

The silkworm moth is a small white moth with a wingspan of about two inches. The female silkworm lays about 500 tiny eggs. The eggs are sticky and yellow. They are about the size of the head of a pin. Once the eggs are laid, the female moth dies.

Silkworm moth

Photo: ManYee DeSandies

What is the difference between worms and caterpillars? Worms are soft-bodied animals that do not change form. Caterpillars are the larva of moths, butterflies, or other insects. They represent one stage in the life cycle of these insects.

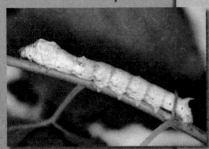

Silkworm caterpillar

Photo: University of Nebraska
Entomology Department

After about 20 days, tiny **caterpillars** crawl out of the eggs. These caterpillars are only about ⅛-inch long. The caterpillars begin to feed on mulberry leaves. This is their only food, and they eat, and eat, and eat. Farmers must keep the caterpillars supplied with fresh chopped leaves.

As the caterpillars eat and eat, they grow and grow. Soon they **outgrow** their skins. They must get rid of these old skins and grow new ones. A new skin forms under the old skin. The caterpillar puffs up its body to **split** the old skin. Then the caterpillar wriggles its way free. This process is called **molting**. Once again, the caterpillar proceeds to feast on mulberry leaves.

The molting process happens four times in the life of a silkworm caterpillar. The caterpillar continues to grow until it weighs more than 10,000 times as much as it did when it emerged from the egg!

When the caterpillar reaches its full size, it stops eating.

Now it is ready to make its cocoon. Special glands, called **silk glands**, have formed inside the silkworm's body. The silkworm has an opening, called a **spinneret**, near its mouth. The silk glands produce a liquid. The silkworm pushes the liquid out through the spinneret. When this liquid meets the air, it hardens into a thread. The silkworm uses the thread to construct a **cocoon** around its body.

The silkworm's cocoon is made of one unbroken fiber. This thread is over one mile long. The silkworm wraps the thread around itself over and over again in a figure-eight pattern. When it has finished, it is completely covered with a thick, dense layer of light-colored silk.

While the silkworm is inside the cocoon, more changes are taking place to its body. The caterpillar becomes a **pupa**. Over the next three weeks, the pupa grows long legs and a short, thick body. Wings, antennae, and compound eyes also form. The pupa changes into a **moth**.

The moth produces a chemical that dissolves the tough silk threads of the cocoon. The moth climbsout through a hole in the cocoon.

This entire process of growth and change is called metamorphosis. **Metamorphosis** is the way that most insects develop.

Photo: ManYee DeSandies

A silkworm is in the process of spinning its cocoon.

Photo: ManYee DeSandies

Inside the cocoon, the caterpillar becomes a pupa.

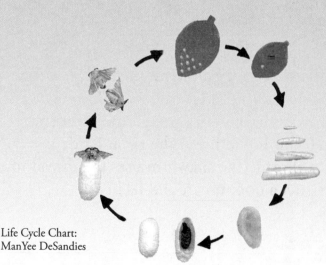

Life Cycle Chart:
ManYee DeSandies

Most silkworm farmers do not want the moths to emerge from the cocoons because this breaks the long fiber into many smaller pieces. So farmers place the cocoons in a hot oven to kill the pupae. Then the cocoons are sent to a **factory** to be processed into silk.

At the factory, the cocoons are washed to remove the sticky substance on the outside of the silk fibers. Unless this sticky substance is washed away, the silk threads will adhere to each other. Then, the silk is unwound from each cocoon.

Photo: University of Nebraska Entomology Department

In Asia, much of the silk processing work is still done by hand.

The fibers from several cocoons are wound together to create a single, thicker filament. These threads are then **dyed** and **woven** into fabric. The fabric is made into clothing, curtains, bedsheets, and other products.

Scientists in Japan are working to create a new kind of silk. They have changed the genes of some silkworms. These silkworms make silk that includes proteins found in the human body. This new silk might be useful in creating skin grafts for people who have been injured or burned.

Questions About
Silkworms

Photo: University of Nebraska
Entomology Department

Fill in the circle that best answers each question.

1. Which of these do silkworms eat?
   - Ⓐ chopped lettuce
   - Ⓑ mulberry leaves
   - Ⓒ seaweed
   - Ⓓ milkweed

2. How many times in their lives do silkworms molt, or shed their skins?
   - Ⓐ one
   - Ⓑ two
   - Ⓒ four
   - Ⓓ three

3. Silk glands and the spinneret function to help the silkworm _____.
   - Ⓐ molt for the last time
   - Ⓑ change into a pupa
   - Ⓒ digest its food
   - Ⓓ spin a silk cocoon

4. If allowed to live out its life cycle, a silkworm emerges from the cocoon as _____.
   - Ⓐ a grasshopper
   - Ⓑ a butterfly
   - Ⓒ a hornet
   - Ⓓ a moth

5. When a silkworm caterpillar reaches its full size, it _____.
   - Ⓐ stops eating
   - Ⓑ stops moving
   - Ⓒ eats more than ever
   - Ⓓ dies

6. *Vegetarian silk* is silk that _____.
   - Ⓐ is made by a process that allows the silkworms to live out their life cycle
   - Ⓑ is made by feeding the silkworms vegetables
   - Ⓒ vegetarians wear
   - Ⓓ is made from cotton

Reading • EMC 4533 • ©2005 by Evan-Moor Corp.

Is It True?

Write a T in front of each statement that is true. Write an F in front of each statement that is false. Rewrite each false statement to make it true.

___ Silkworms are not really worms.

_____

___ Silk might be used to help people who have been burned.

_____

___ A silkworm's cocoon is made of one long continuous fiber.

_____

___ Silkworm moths are the only insects that develop through metamorphosis.

_____

___ Silk begins as a liquid within the body of the silkworm.

_____

___ The female silkworm moth lays about 5 large eggs.

_____

___ The eggs hatch in 30 days.

_____

___ One silk fiber can be a mile long.

_____

Match the Meaning

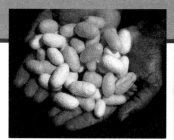

Photo: University of Nebraska
Entomology Department

Find each **bolded** word in the story and read the
sentence in which it is found. Write the letter of the
correct definition on the line in front of each word.

1. _____ **metamorphosis**   5. _____ **moth**

2. _____ **molting**   6. _____ **pupa**

3. _____ **silk glands**   7. _____ **spinneret**

4. _____ **cocoon**   8. _____ **caterpillars**

a. the larvae of insects such as moths and butterflies

b. the process of growth and change that a silkworm experiences

c. a case that the caterpillar constructs around its body

d. the process of replacing old skin with new

e. the adult stage of the silkworm's life cycle

f. the part of a silkworm's body that produces a liquid that becomes silk thread

g. an opening through which liquid from the silk glands leaves the silkworm's body

h. the life cycle stage that comes after the caterpillar stage

                 Reading • EMC 4533 • ©2005 by Evan-Moor Corp.

Which Word Fits?

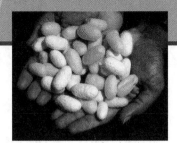

Photo: University of Nebraska
Entomology Department

Complete each sentence using a word from the box. If you nccd hclp with thc mcaning of the words, look for them in the story and read the sentences in which they are found.

spun	outgrow	dyed	vegetarian
split	factory	fabric	woven

1. Jennifer chose a bright blue _____ to make her new skirt.

2. My brother works in a _____ that makes tennis rackets.

3. The lamb's wool was _____ into soft, fluffy yarn.

4. Angie will soon _____ her shoes and need a new pair.

5. The salesperson told us that the yellow scarf was _____ with natural vegetable colors.

6. Jeffrey worked at the loom, making a beautiful _____ coverlet.

7. A _____ does not eat meat.

8. Dad used a large knife to _____ the coconut.

Know Your Roots

Many English words have parts that come from Greek and Latin, two ancient languages. Here are the meanings of some word parts:

ad—to	cred—believe	in—not	fac—make
fila—thread	here—stick	cycl—circular	struct—build
viv—live	meta—change	morph—form, shape	

Using the information in the box, write your best definition of each word. Use a dictionary to check your work.

1. metamorphosis:

_____

2. cycle:

_____

3. adhere:

_____

4. incredible:

_____

5. filament:

_____

6. factory:

_____

7. survive:

_____

8. construct:

_____

The Silkworm Moth Life Cycle

 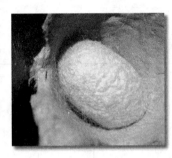 

Using the photos as a guide, explain the life cycle of the silkworm moth.

First, _____

_____

Then, _____

_____

After that, _____

_____

Finally, _____

_____

Joy Adamson: LIVING WITH LIONS

The day that would change Joy Adamson's life forever began like any other. Joy was at home with her husband, George. At that time, George was the senior game **warden** in Kenya, a country in East Africa.

A young African tribesman came to the house to see George. The upset young man was in tears because a lion had killed his brother. The lion had crept into their camp the **previous** night and had dragged the brother into the bush. Tribal members had searched for the missing man all morning. The **gruesome** fact was this: all they could find were his hands and feet.

The man wanted George to track and kill the lion that had eaten his brother. George and Joy set out at once with the tribesman. They set up camp in the area where the attack had taken place. While Joy set up her easel and began to paint, George drove off with another hunter to search for the lion.

At the site of the lion attack, the hunters found lion tracks and followed them up into the hills. Suddenly, a large lioness appeared on a rocky **outcropping**, springing directly into the hunters' path. She growled fiercely at them. It seemed to George that she was about to attack, so he quickly raised his rifle and fired a single accurate shot. The lioness fell to the ground, dead.

As George examined her body, he heard some tiny mewing sounds coming from a crack in the rock outcropping. He reached deep into the crack and pulled out three tiny lion cubs. They were so little that their eyes had not yet opened.

Now George understood why the lioness had been so fierce! She was protecting her babies from human threat. She was not the man-eater he had been seeking. Sadly, he took the three little cubs and drove back to camp.

When George got out of the car with an armful of tiny, squirming baby lions, Joy dropped her paintbrush and immediately took over. Joy had cared for many young animals over the years, but she had never tried to raise baby lions! Nevertheless, she was determined to save these babies. She and George took them home and looked after them.

Reading • EMC 4533 • ©2005 by Evan-Moor Corp.

The lion cubs, all females, grew rapidly. Joy adored the cubs, but she did not want them to become too attached to her and George. They tried to raise the lions as naturally as possible, hoping to someday return them to the wild. They allowed the cubs to roam freely in the woods around their home. But as the lions grew bigger and stronger, Joy and George realized they could not keep three large lions. They decided to present two of the cubs to a zoo; they would keep the smallest cub, which they named Elsa.

Joy and George took Elsa with them on **safaris**. They embarked on lessons to teach her to hunt and to fend for herself. Although Elsa learned quickly, she remained much attached to Joy and George. She slept in their tent at night and sometimes even took naps with Joy in her camp cot.

Elsa liked to play with her human friends, but as Elsa grew to her adult size, this play became dangerous. More than once, Elsa knocked Joy to the ground, biting and scratching her. Joy and George both realized that it was time to find Elsa a new home. They knew she needed a wild home where she could live the life she was born to lead.

It took some time to find the right **location**. Finally, Joy and George decided to release Elsa in Meru Park at the foot of Mt. Kenya. They found a **remote** location and turned Elsa loose. The Adamsons stayed in the area for a time, helping Elsa get food. In time, she learned to hunt for herself and became more and more **independent**.

Joy and George were thrilled when Elsa mated with a wild lion and had three cubs of her own. Now they were certain she would truly become a wild lioness. However, in spite of this success, Elsa never forgot Joy and George. Whenever they camped nearby, Elsa would come to visit, rubbing her head against their legs in greeting.

When her cubs were old enough to travel, Elsa brought them into camp to meet Joy and George. But Joy and George kept their distance from the cubs. They did not want them to get too used to people. They wanted Elsa to be **content** in her new life with her lion family.

Joy missed Elsa, but was happy that she had made a successful life as a wild lion. She believed that Elsa's story was important. Joy wanted to write a book about Elsa, but she was uncertain of her skills as a writer. She asked a friend to write Elsa's story. Her friend encouraged her to write the book herself since Joy was the person who had raised Elsa and who had loved Elsa enough to set her free.

So Joy set up a typewriter and went to work. The book she wrote about Elsa, *Born Free*, became a huge **international** bestseller. Joy traveled all over the world, signing books and giving talks about Elsa. She also talked about the importance of saving the wild animals of the world. She spoke about the need to **preserve** the places in which these animals lived.

A movie about Elsa, also entitled *Born Free,* was made in 1964. The movie was very popular. But some people complained that the movie was not **realistic**. It did not show all the problems and difficulties that Joy and George experienced in their efforts to return Elsa to the wild.

However, the movie brought Elsa's amazing story to the attention of millions of people. It helped many people take a new interest in the survival of the Earth's wild animals.

Joy lived out her life in Africa, working with wild animals. She wrote more books about her experiences. She traveled around the world speaking on behalf of wildlife. She encouraged others to work for conservation. She gave much of the money she made from her books to this cause.

At the age of 70, Joy's life ended tragically. She was murdered by a **poacher** in Meru National Park. But Joy's work lives on. Her heartfelt interest in animals and her great love for Elsa helped inspire a worldwide movement to protect wildlife. For Joy Adamson, there was no greater gift than the beauty and spirit of wild animals, living free.

Questions About
Joy Adamson:
LIVING WITH LIONS

Fill in the circle that best answers each question.

1. George Adamson found three lion cubs _____.
   - (A) huddled in a hollow log
   - (B) crouching under his car
   - (C) hiding in a crack in a rock
   - (D) clinging to the branches of a tree

2. Joy and George let the lions roam freely near their house because they _____.
   - (A) wanted the lions to be as free as possible
   - (B) wanted the lions to scare people away
   - (C) hoped the lions would run away
   - (D) didn't want to care for the lions

3. Joy and George tried to teach Elsa to _____.
   - (A) play ball
   - (B) do circus tricks
   - (C) hunt for her own food
   - (D) attack anyone who bothered them

4. After Elsa was released in the wild, she _____.
   - (A) lived alone and would not interact with other lions
   - (B) often came to visit Joy and George
   - (C) forgot all about Joy and George
   - (D) disappeared

5. Joy wrote a book entitled _____.
   - (A) *Taking Care of Animals*
   - (B) *My Friends, the Lions*
   - (C) *Elsa, the Lioness*
   - (D) *Born Free*

6. Joy traveled the world speaking about the needs of _____.
   - (A) children
   - (B) wild animals
   - (C) artists
   - (D) musicians

Write About the Story

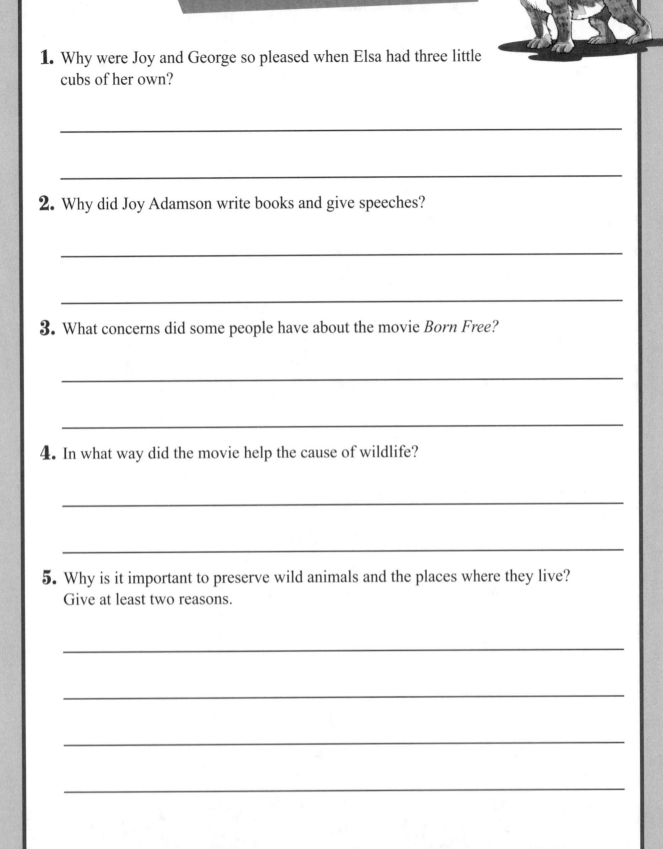

1. Why were Joy and George so pleased when Elsa had three little cubs of her own?

   _____

   _____

2. Why did Joy Adamson write books and give speeches?

   _____

   _____

3. What concerns did some people have about the movie *Born Free?*

   _____

   _____

4. In what way did the movie help the cause of wildlife?

   _____

   _____

5. Why is it important to preserve wild animals and the places where they live? Give at least two reasons.

   _____

   _____

   _____

   _____

Match the Meaning

Find each **bolded** word in the story and read the sentence in which it is found. Write the letter of the correct definition on the line in front of each word.

1. _____ remote

2. _____ international

3. _____ gruesome

4. _____ outcropping

5. _____ previous

6. _____ safaris

7. _____ independent

8. _____ realistic

9. _____ content

10. _____ warden

11. _____ preserve

12. _____ location

13. _____ poacher

a. a ledge of rock that sticks out from its surroundings

b. expeditions; trips

c. free; self-regulating

d. earlier; prior

e. distant; isolated

f. protect; save

g. place

h. truthful; sensible

i. global; worldwide

j. custodian; supervisor

k. happy; satisfied

l. horrible; grisly

m. someone who hunts illegally

Figure Out the Meaning

1. Joy and George taught Elsa to hunt her own food and **fend** for herself.

Fend means _____ .

2. The hunters went to the **site** of the attack to try to find the lion.

Site means _____ .

3. When she reached her **adult** size, Elsa was big and strong.

Adult means _____ .

4. The **survival** of wild animals depends upon human protection.

Survival means _____ .

5. Because she loved animals so much, Joy was **determined** to save the lion cubs.

Determined means _____ .

6. The Adamsons **embarked on** a program to make the young lions independent.

Embarked on means _____ .

Adverbs with -ly

Adverbs tell when, where, why, or how something happens. Many adverbs end with the suffix –ly.

Fill in each blank with an adverb from the box.

suddenly	fiercely	finally	quickly
truly	tragically	sadly	freely

1. The large shaggy dog growled _____ at the burglar.

2. We wanted to get through with our chores _____ so we could go outside and play.

3. Hannah whimpered _____ as fat tears rolled down her cheeks.

4. The unexpected thunderstorm appeared _____.

5. _____, many people were killed by the hurricane.

6. Ron gave _____ of his time because he wanted to help the children.

7. Jesse felt _____ sorry for his mistake.

8. After practicing for days, Marie _____ learned to ride her bike.

Reading • EMC 4533 • ©2005 by Evan-Moor Corp.

Find the Verbs

Verbs are words that describe action.

In each group of four words below, three are verbs that mean about the same thing. One word is not a verb. Circle the word that is <u>not</u> a verb.

wander roam hiker amble	protest laughter complain grumble
help support encourage heart	free release bird let go
seek search detective hunt	preserve protect defend wilderness
attack fighter assault strike	observe examine microscope study

Look at the 8 words you circled. All are _____.

adjectives   nouns   adverbs   prepositions

OLD BRAGWYNN *the* PIRATE

Old Bragwynn the Pirate was the most **dastardly villain** to ever roam the seas. At least, that is what he told everyone who would listen.

When Bragwynn docked his boat and entered some coastal haunt, he set about to brag of his exploits. "Of all the passengers on all the ships I have taken, not a single one remains alive!" he boasted. It wasn't exactly false. It was just that Old Bragwynn had never taken a ship before. Thus, he had not yet had the opportunity to decide on the fate of a passenger.

Bragwynn had spent many days out at sea, most of them paddling around in his rowboat with his dog, One-Eyed Jack. Jack, it should be noted, had two perfectly good eyes. The reason for his name was unknown, even to the old pirate. Sometimes, the pair would spot a ship and row toward it with the intention of commandeering the vessel. The ships, however, always seemed to be heading in the wrong direction.

No matter how hard Old Bragwynn rowed, or how hard the wind blew into his little makeshift sail (which consisted of a broomstick and an old bedsheet), he could never get close enough to get aboard. Bragwynn concluded that the sea goddesses must be against him. The inferiority of his vessel never occurred to him.

 Reading • EMC 4533 • ©2005 by Evan-Moor Corp.

When they were not rowing about, Old Bragwynn and Jack spent their time looking for suitable places to hide their treasure. Of course, they had no treasure. But Bragwynn hoped they would.

Jack seemed to think that the yard right by their seaside shanty was a perfect place to bury this treasure. Jack persisted in digging holes there long after the old pirate had ruled it out as a possibility. It was far too obvious to hide treasure so near to home. Besides, once they had a sizable seagoing ship, Bragwynn had no intention of ever returning to his shack.

There was a small island about a quarter mile from shore. The pirate thought this island was the best place to bury future treasure. He had studied the island in detail and found several locations that seemed just right for hiding loot.

For many years, One-Eyed Jack and Bragwynn spent their waking hours rowing about or making maps of the island. It wasn't until the man and dog had grown quite gray that their luck finally changed.

While out at sea one afternoon, they spotted a ship. It was a large ship, the kind they had failed to catch so many times before. But this time, it appeared that the ship was heading directly for them. There was no way they could miss it.

Bragwynn began rowing as hard as he could, stopping briefly to replace his mop-handle flagpole that Jack kept knocking over with his tail. Soon, the great ship was very near. Bragwynn stopped rowing and clambered onto the bow of the rowboat, nearly **capsizing** the vessel on several occasions.

"Halt!" he shouted, managing to **stabilize** himself on the shifting bow. "Halt! Prepare to be boarded by the most dastardly pirate to ever sail the seas."

The crew aboard the great ship did not even notice the little rowboat in the water just ahead of them. Bragwynn's cries were swallowed by the noise of the wind in the sails and the sea rushing by.

Bragwynn turned to Jack to see what he made of the situation. As he did, the rowboat was smashed into pieces by the great vessel. This would have been the end of the old sea-goer were it not for a sailor who spotted him splashing about.

"Man in the water!" shouted the mate. "Man in the water!"

A ladder was lowered down. Holding Jack in one arm, Bragwynn climbed aboard the ship. Rather than uttering heartfelt thanks, the just-rescued scalawag let loose with a bloodcurdling yell.

"Listen, you scurvy lot! You have been boarded by Old Bragwynn, the most dastardly pirate to ever sail the seas. Bring me your captain so that he may **surrender**, else you all shall meet with a cruel and violent end at the point of my sword!"

As he spoke, he pulled a small, crooked stick from his ragged waistband, twirling it about as though it were a flashing sword.

The absurdity of the situation was too much for the crew. A burst of guffaws erupted from the group. "Why, the old man's a nut," one of them murmured.

"He thinks the stick is a sword," laughed another.

These comments only served to inflame Bragwynn's rage.

"Why, you cowardly scum!" he exploded. "Is your captain not man enough to come before me and face my judgment? Jack, tie them up now. We shall throw them overboard one by one until the captain comes forward!"

Again came a swell of laughter from the crew. "Why, the old salt is telling his dog to tie us up!"

Suddenly, a voice boomed through the crowd. "Enough!" the voice exclaimed. A huge bearded man made his way to the center of the group. His powerful voice matched his barrel chest and the confident set of his shoulders. In his eye was a twinkle that was not exactly friendly.

"I am the captain of this vessel, but I see that you are a greater captain than I. Perhaps we can reach an agreement that will preserve my life." The captain gave a wink to his men as he spoke.

"I do not make deals," declared Bragwynn. "My demands are always met. However, I am willing to listen. Go ahead."

"Ah, a just man," said the captain. "But did you happen to notice that you have laid siege to a fellow pirate? That breaks the **pact** of the thieves of the high seas," the captain stated. He pointed to the Jolly Roger snapping at the top of the mast.

Bragwynn, of course, had not noticed. "Certainly I noticed!" he blustered. "But pacts, like rules, are meant to be broken. I am the dastardliest pirate ever to sail the seas. It is only natural that I should be the first to do so!"

"Oh, indeed, indeed!" replied the captain. "That is why I concluded you were the greater pirate in the first place." The captain paused and removed his hat before going on. "I will surrender control of my ship to you, if you will spare the lives of my men and me. For my part, I will gladly accept a **demotion** and serve as your first mate. What say you? You will need a crew, and you are not likely to find a better one than this."

The captain winked again at his men, who were doing their best to **stifle** their chuckles.

"It is not my custom to spare the lives of those I capture," Bragwynn explained, "but I see the **logic** of your argument. I believe you will be a fine first mate. Therefore, I will break my own rule and spare your lives."

"Ah, very good, sir," the captain exclaimed. "Now, rest here a bit while I tidy up the captain's quarters. I shall soon return to show you to your new **lodgings**."

"Very well," Bragwynn said. He beamed with pride as he sat down atop a barrel to rest.

The captain quickly went below deck and removed the door to his quarters from its hinges. He summoned two crewmen and instructed them to hold the door at the side of the ship. He sent another man to summon Old Bragwynn.

"Right this way, sir," he said to Bragwynn as he approached.

Bragwynn walked smartly up to the door and stood for a moment. "At last," he sighed, "my own command. My own chambers."

He happily pushed the door open, took one step forward, and plunged instantly into the sea.

As for Jack, he stayed aboard and lived the life of a true pirate dog to the end of his days.

Questions About
OLD BRAGWYNN *the* PIRATE

Fill in the circle that best answers each question.

1. Which words best describe Old Bragwynn?
   - Ⓐ dastardly and villainous
   - Ⓑ delusional and nutty
   - Ⓒ capable and crafty
   - Ⓓ smart and witty

2. Which words best describe the captain?
   - Ⓐ welcoming and kindhearted
   - Ⓑ understanding and tolerant
   - Ⓒ jolly and friendly
   - Ⓓ shrewd and ruthless

3. What is a *Jolly Roger*?
   - Ⓐ a pirate flag with skull and crossbones
   - Ⓑ another way of saying "walk the plank"
   - Ⓒ the name of the pirate ship
   - Ⓓ the funniest of the pirates

4. What did Bragwynn order Jack to do?
   - Ⓐ bite the captain
   - Ⓑ howl at the moon
   - Ⓒ tie up the sailors
   - Ⓓ jump into the water

5. Where did Bragwynn think he was going when he stepped through the door?
   - Ⓐ into his new captain's quarters
   - Ⓑ back to his own boat
   - Ⓒ into the bathroom
   - Ⓓ into the kitchen

6. What became of Jack?
   - Ⓐ He jumped into the water to try to save his master.
   - Ⓑ He floated away in the rowboat.
   - Ⓒ He died of a broken heart.
   - Ⓓ He stayed on the pirate ship.

Reading • EMC 4533 • ©2005 by Evan-Moor Corp.

The Reason Is...

Complete each sentence to explain why certain events happened in the story.

1. Bragwynn had never been able to capture a ship because

_____

_____

2. The sailors on the big ship laughed at Bragwynn because

_____

3. The ship's captain offered Bragwynn command of his ship because

_____

4. The captain winked at his crew because

_____

5. Bragwynn boasted about his exploits because

_____

_____

Match the Meaning

Find each **bolded** word in the story and read the sentence
in which it is found. Write the letter of the correct definition
on the line in front of each word.

1. _____ villain

2. _____ capsizing

3. _____ surrender

4. _____ demotion

5. _____ pact

6. _____ stifle

7. _____ dastardly

8. _____ lodgings

9. _____ logic

10. _____ stabilize

a. housing; a place to stay

b. overturning

c. a criminal or bad person

d. to make strong and steady

e. to give up

f. reasoning

g. mean and cruel

h. a reduction in status or rank

i. hold back; stop

j. deal; agreement

Choose two of the words and use each in a sentence.

_____

_____

_____

Words for *Said*

As you read the dialog in this story, you will notice that many different words are used in place of the word said.

- Find at least 6 of these words in the story and write them on the lines below.

_____

_____

_____

_____

_____

_____

- Write a short dialog between two of the characters in the story. Do not use the word *said* in your dialog. Be sure to use quotation marks around the words being spoken.

_____

_____

_____

_____

_____

_____

Two Words Put Together

Compound words are words that are made up of two other words.

There are several compound words in this story. Here are a few of them:

rowboat   flagpole   seaside

Combine the words in the box to create as many compound words as you can. You may use words more than once.

sea	birth	time	water	life	room	line
sun	day	home	over	shore	beam	foot
stick	ball	waist	band	moon	shine	free
fall	step	coat	made	style	broom	board

_____   _____

_____   _____

_____   _____

_____   _____

_____   _____

_____   _____

_____   _____

Buried Treasure

Use the map and the directions to find the spot where the
pirate treasure is buried.

The treasure is buried under a rock.
The treasure is buried north of the Palm Tree Grove.
The treasure is buried east of the Raging River.
The treasure is buried west of Skull Rock.
The treasure is buried south of Poison Pond.
The treasure is buried north and east of Misery Mountain.
The treasure is buried on a shoreline.
Mark an **X** on the spot where the treasure is buried!

KANGAROO ALMANAC

More than 200 years ago, English explorers arrived on the shore of Australia. They were astonished to see large mammals hopping about as if on springs! It is easy to imagine their surprise at these **unlikely** animals. Today, kangaroos continue to fascinate and amaze us.

There are more than 50 different kinds of kangaroos. They come in a variety of sizes from tiny to tall. The rat-kangaroo is the smallest and weighs only about a pound. The largest, the red kangaroo, can stand as tall as a man and weigh 200 pounds. Male kangaroos continue to grow throughout their lives.

Australia

Kangaroos live on the continent of Australia and a few nearby islands. They live in all kinds of **habitats**. The large red kangaroos live on grassy, open plains. Grey kangaroos live in **scrubby** woodlands. Rock wallabies, small kangaroo cousins, make their homes on rocky ledges.

There are even kangaroos that live in trees! These kangaroos have large forearms and small feet. They need stronger arms for climbing.

Reading • EMC 4533 • ©2005 by Evan-Moor Corp.

Pocket Babies

All kangaroos are **marsupials**. Marsupials are a family of mammals whose babies develop in pouches on the mothers' bodies. When a baby kangaroo is born, it is about the size of a jelly bean! The tiny hairless baby wiggles through its mother's fur and crawls into the "pocket" on the front of her body. This pocket, called a **pouch**, will be the baby's home for the next several months. Blind and helpless, the little baby kangaroo, or **joey**, **nestles** in the pouch, drinking milk and growing.

You might think that the joey would be in danger of falling out of the pouch, but this is not true. Strong muscles surround the pouch. The mother kangaroo can use these muscles to close the pouch, making it snug and safe. She can also relax these muscles, making it possible for the baby to climb in and out.

As the joey **matures**, it becomes more independent. It pokes its head out of the mother's pouch and takes a look around the world. Soon, the joey is big enough to hop out of the pouch and move around on its own. But any sign of danger will send the baby scrambling back to the safety of the pouch. Most joeys continue to spend at least part of their time inside the pouch until they are almost a year old. Even after a joey is too large to fit in the pouch, it will stay with the mother for several more months.

Hop, Hop, Hooray!

Kangaroos move by hopping. They have very large back legs and feet. These legs are extremely strong and muscular. They also have large flexible tails. A dense bundle of tendons connect the tail with the hipbones. These muscles and tendons enable the kangaroo to hop with enormous power. The larger kangaroos can cover more than 20 feet with each hop. They can cruise along easily at the speed of 20 miles per hour. And they can reach a top speed of over 50 miles per hour!

Kangaroo Karate

While they look cute and cuddly, it is important to remember that kangaroos are wild animals. If they feel threatened, they may attack. Males often fight with each other, sometimes as a form of social play. They can kick with their powerful hind feet and punch with their forearms.

Kangaroos can be dangerous to people, too. Some people have been badly injured by kangaroos. Australian wildlife officials caution people never to feed or approach kangaroos.

Reading • EMC 4533 • ©2005 by Evan-Moor Corp.

'Roo Food

Kangaroos are **herbivores**. This means they eat vegetation, such as grasses and shrubs. Sometimes, they will also eat fruits and berries. Most kangaroos prefer tender green shoots and leaves that have more protein and are easier to digest.

Kangaroo Survival

Some kangaroos are endangered, while others number in the millions. Predators, including foxes and wildcats, threaten some smaller kangaroo species. **Dingoes**, the wild dogs of Australia, once kept populations of larger kangaroos in check. But sheep ranchers have killed many dingoes in order to protect their sheep.

The sheep ranches that cover much of the Australian countryside are good homes for kangaroos. Kangaroos drink the water that ranchers provide for their sheep. They enjoy the sweet grasses that ranchers grow for their sheep. Of course, the sheep ranchers are not always happy to share with the kangaroos.

In addition to taking food and water, kangaroos often cause damage by digging holes and knocking down fences. For sheep ranchers, the kangaroo is simply a pest.

The Australian government wants to protect ranch land. It also wants to prevent the **overpopulation** of kangaroos. To meet these goals, the government allows people to kill some kangaroos. Shooters go out at night and use lights to spot the kangaroos. The hides are used to make leather, and the meat is used for food.

This may seem very cruel, but it is necessary to prevent overpopulation. If the kangaroo population is allowed to grow too large, there will not be enough food for all the kangaroos, and many will starve. Also, when animal populations become overcrowded, disease spreads more easily. Hunting helps prevent these problems and keep the kangaroo population healthy.

Kangaroo Coolers

The climate in many parts of Australia is quite hot. Kangaroos have several methods for keeping cool. They rest during the heat of the day, coming out to feed in the evening and early morning.

Kangaroos pant to allow heat to escape from their bodies. They breathe very rapidly when they pant—up to 300 times per minute. While panting, they also drool. The saliva wets their forearms, which have many blood vessels just under the skin. As air passes over the wet fur of their forearms, heat is carried away.

Kangaroos are good diggers. They will dig **shallow** beds in the cool soil under a shady tree. Sometimes they will even dig several feet into the earth to find water.

Kangaroo Lingo

You know that a baby kangaroo is called a joey. A male kangaroo is called a **buck**. A female kangaroo is called a **doe**. A group of kangaroos is called a **mob**.

'Roos in Zoos

Kangaroos live in **captivity** in zoos around the world. The largest group of kangaroos outside of Australia can be found in the Kangaroo Conservation Center near Atlanta, Georgia.

Daily tours allow visitors to see and photograph kangaroos without traveling all the way to Australia. The goal of the Kangaroo Conservation Center is to help people learn about kangaroos and other Australian animals. In 2002, the Kangaroo Conservation Center won an award for its tree kangaroo **conservation** program.

Questions About
KANGAROO ALMANAC

Fill in the circle that best answers each question.

1. Kangaroos are native to which of these continents?
   Ⓐ Asia
   Ⓑ Europe
   Ⓒ Antarctica
   Ⓓ Australia

2. In which U.S. state can you find the largest collection of kangaroos outside Australia?
   Ⓐ Iowa
   Ⓑ New York
   Ⓒ Georgia
   Ⓓ California

3. Which of these is <u>not</u> a way kangaroos keep cool?
   Ⓐ They pant rapidly.
   Ⓑ They hop into a billabong.
   Ⓒ They wet their forearms with saliva.
   Ⓓ They dig a hole in the cool dirt under a tree.

4. Which statement tells about newborn kangaroos?
   Ⓐ They look like jelly beans.
   Ⓑ They are tiny and hairless.
   Ⓒ They are born in the mother's pouch.
   Ⓓ They are able to hop soon after birth.

5. In which way can kangaroos be dangerous to people?
   Ⓐ They can kick and punch.
   Ⓑ They can claw and bite.
   Ⓒ They can knock a person over with their tails.
   Ⓓ They can dig holes and knock down fences.

6. What is the top speed of a large kangaroo?
   Ⓐ about 10 miles per hour
   Ⓑ about 20 miles per hour
   Ⓒ about 50 miles per hour
   Ⓓ about 100 miles per hour

Write About the Story

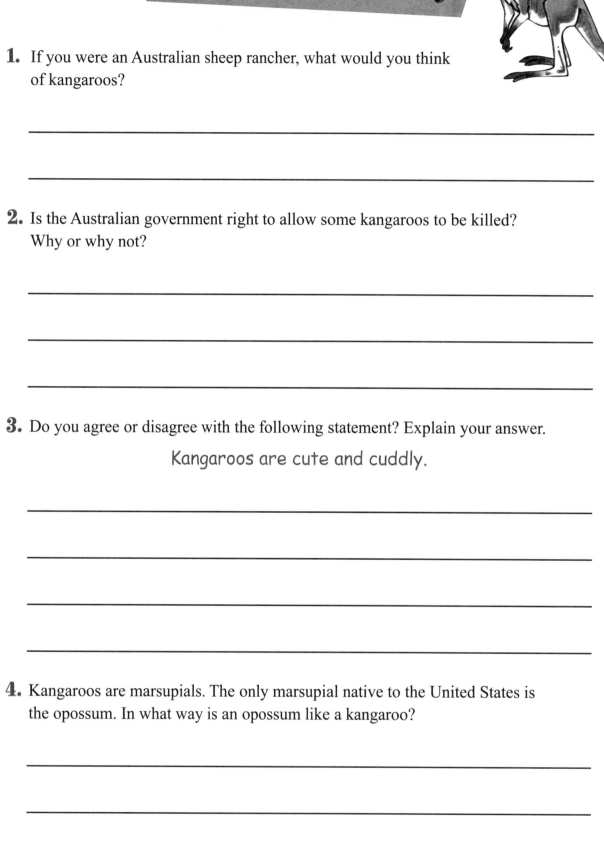

1. If you were an Australian sheep rancher, what would you think of kangaroos?

   _____

   _____

2. Is the Australian government right to allow some kangaroos to be killed? Why or why not?

   _____

   _____

   _____

3. Do you agree or disagree with the following statement? Explain your answer.

   Kangaroos are cute and cuddly.

   _____

   _____

   _____

   _____

4. Kangaroos are marsupials. The only marsupial native to the United States is the opossum. In what way is an opossum like a kangaroo?

   _____

   _____

   _____

Choose the Right Meaning

Find these highlighted words in the story. Read the sentence in which each word is found. Choose the correct meaning.

1. A **dingo** is _____.
   - Ⓐ a wild pig
   - Ⓑ a wild dog
   - Ⓒ a wild horse
   - Ⓓ a wild cat

2. The word **conservation** means _____.
   - Ⓐ care and protection
   - Ⓑ a meeting of a group
   - Ⓒ a talk between several people
   - Ⓓ changing of water vapor to liquid water

3. A **habitat** is _____.
   - Ⓐ a kind of clothing for animals
   - Ⓑ the covering of an animal's skin
   - Ⓒ the way a certain kind of animal moves
   - Ⓓ the environment in which a particular animal lives

4. A **scrubby** tree is _____.
   - Ⓐ tall
   - Ⓑ dried up
   - Ⓒ dying
   - Ⓓ undersized

5. An animal in **captivity** would <u>not</u> be in _____.
   - Ⓐ a zoo
   - Ⓑ a cage
   - Ⓒ a forest
   - Ⓓ a pen

6. Where might you **nestle**?
   - Ⓐ in your bed
   - Ⓑ on a bench
   - Ⓒ in the shower
   - Ⓓ at the gym

7. In this story, the word **matures** means _____.
   - Ⓐ becomes ripe
   - Ⓑ acts grownup
   - Ⓒ grows to adulthood
   - Ⓓ due and payable, like a loan

8. Which word below is an antonym for **shallow**?
   - Ⓐ thin
   - Ⓑ deep
   - Ⓒ low
   - Ⓓ slender

9. The word **unlikely** means _____.
   - Ⓐ improbable
   - Ⓑ disliked
   - Ⓒ not friendly
   - Ⓓ not the same

10. If there is an **overpopulation** of something, _____.
    - Ⓐ there are not enough of the thing
    - Ⓑ the thing is too popular
    - Ⓒ the thing costs too much
    - Ⓓ there are too many of the thing

Which Word Fits?

Some of the bolded words in the story refer to kangaroos. Write the correct bolded word in each sentence below.

1. The female kangaroo waited patiently as her young _____ explored the nearby area.

2. _____ are a group of mammals whose newborn babies live and grow for several months in the mother's

_____.

3. Kangaroos are like cows and deer in that they eat plants. They are

_____.

4. The _____ of kangaroos grazed on the tender spring grasses.

5. The young male kangaroo invited another _____ to play fight.

6. A kangaroo _____ will protect her joey.

Fact or Opinion?

A fact tells information that is true.

An opinion tells about someone's thoughts or feelings.

Write **fact** or **opinion** after each statement.

1. Kangaroos are cute. _____

2. There are many different kinds of kangaroos. _____

3. Kangaroos live in Australia. _____

4. Kangaroos move by hopping. _____

5. Some kangaroos live in trees. _____

6. People should never kill kangaroos. _____

7. Kangaroos are herbivores. _____

8. Kangaroos make good pets. _____

9. Everyone should visit the zoo to see kangaroos. _____

10. Kangaroos sometimes dig holes to find water. _____

Write one fact and one opinion of your own. Ask a family member to tell which is which.

_____

_____

_____

_____

Which Spelling Is Correct?

Circle the correct spelling for each word.

1.	safty	safety	saftey
2.	island	iland	islind
3.	neccessary	necessary	necessery
4.	excape	escape	esscape
5.	million	milion	milliun
6.	aminal	annimal	animal
7.	suprise	surprize	surprise
8.	immagine	amagine	imagine
9.	diffrent	different	differant
10.	government	goverment	governmant

Write sentences using the correct spellings of three words from the list above.

1. _____

   _____

2. _____

   _____

3. _____

   _____

   Reading • EMC 4533 • ©2005 by Evan-Moor Corp.

How Shalbus Egbert Bested The Bear

Deep in the darkest forest, there are many creatures well known to humankind. There are bears, birds, squirrels and deer, along with foxes, badgers, snakes, and salamanders. But there are also those creatures unknown to all but a few men and women, and whose very existence is doubted by most. Among these creatures are the pixies.

Pixies are small, usually less than six inches tall. Except for their small **stature**, pixies look very much like humans. They always wear green because their clothes are made of leaves. Their heads are **adorned** with small caps woven from stems and pine needles. Shy and swift, pixies usually hide when they hear someone approaching. This is why so few humans know of them.

The most famous pixie that ever lived was called Shalbus Egbert. Now, pixies love to sing, and Shalbus was a great singer. Pixies love to dance, and Shalbus was a graceful dancer. Pixies love to drink root beer, and Shalbus was a master brewer. Pixies love to eat, and Shalbus was a very fine cook. But none of these **attributes** were the reason that Shalbus Egbert won his fame. No, Shalbus won his fame because of the tales he told of his great adventures.

The winters were the most difficult time for the pixies. Seeking shelter from the elements, the pixies would sit **huddled** underground beneath the roots of a tree. For days at a time, they would sit in their burrows, drifting in and out of sleep. The first days were not so bad, as there was food and drink, and so there was song. But as the supplies disappeared, so did their **glee**. One day seemed to fall into another. Life became dull and **monotonous**. Without the stories of Shalbus Egbert, the long cold winter would have been unbearable for them. These stories were the source of their pleasure until the coming of spring with all its incredible wonders. (Spring, naturally, was the pixies' favorite time of year.)

The most popular tale that Shalbus recounted was the tale of how he bested the bear. At the mention of this story, the jaws of the young pixies would drop.

"No!" they would squeal in disbelief. "How could a pixie best a bear? A bear is so big, and we pixies are so small!"

"Be silent and listen, and I will tell you if you really want to know," Shalbus would solemnly reply.

Then the room would grow quiet. The snoring pixies would be nudged awake by their neighbors so that no one would miss the great tale that all had been waiting eagerly to hear.

"When I was much younger, I used to **venture** out into the woods," began Shalbus. "One day, I **strayed** farther than usual from the great tree, which we sit under now. I came upon a bush that was heavily **laden** with fruits. I tasted of these fruits, and indeed, they were delicious purple bumbleberries. I wanted to share them with the rest of my friends and family. I began trying to think of a plan that would enable me to bring some home. I found a great leaf from a linden tree. I thought I could use it to drag some berries home. I began to pull the berries down and set them on the leaf. Just as I was becoming exhausted, and my leaf was getting quite full, I felt a great rumbling beneath my feet.

"I looked up just in time to see a bear approaching rapidly. As any sensible pixie would do, I leapt for cover under the bush. The bear, I believe, could smell that I was near, but being a bear, he was not too concerned about the scent of a pixie. I was not too concerned either at that point. My plan was to simply wait until the bear had eaten his fill and left. Then I would take my berries home. And this is what I would have done, had the bear not noticed the nice pile of berries that I had worked so hard to collect.

"As he turned his great head in their direction and stooped down to scoop them into his greedy mouth, I could stand it no longer. I leapt out from my hiding place and began to shout at the bear. 'Listen you dreadful creature. I've worked hard to make that pile of berries, and I mean to bring them home. They're mine! Do you hear me?'

"The bear snapped his head around sharply and let out a mighty roar. At that moment, I realized what a foolish thing I had done by coming out of my hiding place. I could very well have lost my life over a pile of berries! But fortunately my mind worked quickly, and I came up with a plan.

'Hear this, Bear,' I began. 'There is no need for us to **quarrel**. The simple truth is that there are enough berries here to satisfy us both.' The bear inched closer with a hungry look in his eyes. I could see what he was thinking: it would be easier to eat me and my berries, than to hassle with pulling the others from the bush. So naturally, seeing it as my only hope of survival, I made him an offer.

'You go lie in that nice sunny patch of grass, Bear. I will pull berries from the bush for you. In fact, I promise to pull them from the bush until you are full! You won't have to do a lick of work!'

"This, I knew, was an offer a rather lazy and greedy bear could not refuse. Although I was exhausted from the day's hard work already behind me, I set to the task once again. I filled up leaf after leaf with the berries. I laid each leaf before the big beast, who swallowed it down in one quick gulp. Soon, I realized that I was in trouble. I had agreed to serve the beast until he was full, and he had just eaten what would have been a feast for an entire village of pixies as though it were a mere **morsel**. I attempted to **renegotiate** my position.

'Bear, there is no way I can serve you until you are full. Your belly is far too great. Let me go in peace, and you may have the rest of the berries on the bush. I won't take one more so long as I live. I will even give you the berries that I picked earlier today. I am now far too exhausted to be able to bring them back home.'

"But the bear was uninterested. He showed his teeth to me once more, letting me know that I would not be leaving with my life until his **appetite** was **assuaged**.

"My situation was terribly **daunting**. I could not continue to pick berries. My arms felt as though they were about to come off. I was simply incapable of fulfilling the demands of the much larger animal. I was about to despair, and glanced around wildly seeking some avenue of escape.

"By chance, my eye fell upon a solution to my problem! Only a few feet away from the bumbleberry patch stood a different bush, small and almost **insignificant** in comparison. In fact, I had not even noticed it until that moment. That was a rootleberry bush, the berries of which are very poisonous. Whoever eats from the rootleberry bush falls into a deep, unpleasant sleep and awakens hours later with an **agonizing** headache. Perhaps, just perhaps, I could get enough of these berries into the bear to make my getaway.

"Remembering the way the **brute** had simply swallowed down the last batch of berries, I was sure that if I could mix some of these dangerous berries in with the bumbleberries, he would gulp them down without a thought.

"I took a deep breath to renew my strength and ran over to the rootleberry bush and picked all the fat red berries I could reach. I set the berries on a great leaf and covered them carefully with a **heap** of bumbleberries. Then, once more, I laid the leaf before the bear. Just as he had done before, he gulped down my offering and demanded more. For a moment, I feared that my plan had come to **naught**.

"But in the next instant, the poison took effect. The bear's face took on a funny expression, his mouth began to foam, and his eyes grew red and crossed as he fell to the ground with a thud. Not knowing how long the bear would sleep, and not wanting to be near when he awoke with a thumping head, I **scampered** away as fast as ever my pixie legs could carry me. I didn't stop until I was safely back in this very burrow under this very tree."

"And that is the story, my young pixies, of how I, Shalbus Egbert, defeated a mighty bear."

The pixies began to applaud wildly. The story of the bear was all any of them talked of...at least until Shalbus began his next story.

Questions About
How Shalbus Egbert Bested the Bear

Fill in the circle that best answers each question.

1. Shalbus was famous mostly for his _____.
   Ⓐ graceful dancing
   Ⓑ singing ability
   Ⓒ brewing of root beer
   Ⓓ storytelling ability

2. The pixies disliked winter because _____.
   Ⓐ the long cold winter days were dull and boring for them
   Ⓑ their clothes were not warm enough
   Ⓒ it was crowded underground
   Ⓓ it was too hard to sleep

3. Shalbus met a great bear when he was out picking _____.
   Ⓐ blackberries
   Ⓑ lingonberries
   Ⓒ bumbleberries
   Ⓓ rootleberries

4. What did Shalbus plan to do with the berries he picked?
   Ⓐ Take them home to share with the other pixies.
   Ⓑ Give them to his grandmother.
   Ⓒ Eat them up all by himself.
   Ⓓ Feed them to the birds.

5. Shalbus wanted the bear to eat rootleberries because they _____.
   Ⓐ were so delicious
   Ⓑ would kill the bear
   Ⓒ would fill up the bear's stomach
   Ⓓ would make the bear go to sleep

6. How did Shalbus trick the bear into eating the rootleberries?
   Ⓐ He mixed them into a tasty drink.
   Ⓑ He hid them under a pile of bumbleberries.
   Ⓒ He told the bear they were bumbleberries.
   Ⓓ He slipped them into the bear's mouth while the bear was sleeping.

About the Pixies

1. Why are the pixies cheered by the stories Shalbus Egbert tells?

_____

_____

2. How do you think the young pixies feel about Shalbus?

_____

_____

3. Circle three words below that you think describe Shalbus. Write a
   short paragraph using evidence from the story to justify your choices.

generous   brave   outgoing   clever   mean   adventurous   lazy

_____

_____

_____

_____

_____

_____

_____

Choose the Right Meaning

Find these highlighted words in the story. Read the sentence in which each word is found. Choose the correct meaning.

1. The word **stature** means _____.
   - Ⓐ monument
   - Ⓑ bridge
   - Ⓒ height
   - Ⓓ color

2. The word **huddled** means _____.
   - Ⓐ lost
   - Ⓑ frightened
   - Ⓒ joined hands
   - Ⓓ crowded together

3. The word **renegotiate** means _____.
   - Ⓐ to explain
   - Ⓑ to change
   - Ⓒ to convince
   - Ⓓ to bargain again

4. The word **laden** means _____.
   - Ⓐ overloaded
   - Ⓑ cheerful
   - Ⓒ soggy
   - Ⓓ stinky

5. The word **assuaged** means _____.
   - Ⓐ complained
   - Ⓑ satisfied
   - Ⓒ forgotten
   - Ⓓ injured

6. The word **agonizing** means _____.
   - Ⓐ very funny
   - Ⓑ rather mild
   - Ⓒ extremely painful
   - Ⓓ somewhat embarrassing

7. The word **glee** means _____.
   - Ⓐ sleepiness
   - Ⓑ sorrow
   - Ⓒ anger
   - Ⓓ joy

8. The word **strayed** means _____.
   - Ⓐ wandered
   - Ⓑ leapt
   - Ⓒ crept
   - Ⓓ poured

9. The word **insignificant** means _____.
   - Ⓐ large and beautiful
   - Ⓑ not important
   - Ⓒ shiny
   - Ⓓ soft

10. The word **heap** means _____.
    - Ⓐ a pile
    - Ⓑ a pound
    - Ⓒ a basket
    - Ⓓ a string

Reading • EMC 4533 • ©2005 by Evan-Moor Corp.

Match the Meaning

Find these **bolded** words in the story. Read the sentence in which each word is found. Write the letter of the correct definition on the line in front of each word.

1. _____ adorned

2. _____ attributes

3. _____ monotonous

4. _____ quarrel

5. _____ morsel

6. _____ appetite

7. _____ daunting

8. _____ brute

9. _____ naught

10. _____ scampered

a. nothing

b. overwhelming

c. argue

d. qualities

e. beast

f. repetitive and boring

g. desire for food

h. a tiny piece

i. decorated

j. ran quickly

Fluency:
Reading with Expression

To be a good storyteller like Shalbus, it is important to use appropriate expression.

Read the following passage aloud three times. Let your voice rise and fall to show emotion. Use different voices for the characters.

One morning, all the young pixies gathered around Shalbus Egbert.

"Please, Mr. Egbert, please tell us a story," they cried.

"Perhaps a little later," replied Shalbus, not unkindly. "I am cleaning the burrow this morning, and I must finish polishing the tree roots and dusting all the pebbles."

One bold little pixie named Susie shyly crept up to the famous storyteller and whispered in his pointy ear.

"If we help you clean the burrow, then will you tell us a story?" she asked sweetly.

"Yes, yes!" shouted all the other little pixies. "We will gladly do the cleaning if only you will favor us with a story."

At this, Shalbus Egbert began to laugh.

"Ho, ho, my little friends. How can I turn down such a fine offer as this! You clean the burrow, and I will think of a brand new story to tell you!"

So the little pixies set to work in a frenzy, dusting and polishing, polishing and dusting. As soon as they were finished, Shalbus Egbert settled himself in a comfy chair in a cozy corner of the burrow, and the little pixies gathered round. Their brown eyes shone with anticipation as Shalbus Egbert began his tale.

"Once upon a time, when I was just a wee little pixie like yourselves...."

 Reading • EMC 4533 • ©2005 by Evan-Moor Corp.

Prefixes That Mean "Not"

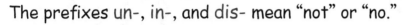

The prefixes un-, in-, and dis- mean "not" or "no."

The word box below contains words from the story that have the prefixes un-, in-, or dis-.

Use one of the words to complete each sentence.

unknown	incapable	unpleasant	incredible
disbelief	disappeared	unbearable	
uninterested	insignificant		

1. My cousin told us an _____ story about a large green monster.

2. Janet was completely _____ in our discussion about fashion trends.

3. Jose said the pain from his toothache was almost _____.

4. Susan's dog slipped out of his collar and _____ into the woods.

5. The medicine tasted very _____.

6. Scientists have discovered a planet that was previously _____.

7. Please include all important facts in your report, but do not include

_____ details.

8. When Jake won the prize, his first reaction was _____.

9. Larissa was _____ of moving the heavy chair by herself.

ABNER THE CROW & Tawb the Snake

One sunny day, Abner the Crow was sitting on his usual perch on the highest branch of an **ancient** oak tree overlooking the forest floor. As he gazed **idly** about, he noticed an unusual sight. Tawb, the old snake who lived in a den at the foot of Abner's tree, had left his hole. He was **slithering** quietly along the forest floor. Now, this was unusual because Tawb almost never left the **comfort** of his hole. In fact, he was known far and wide for his extreme laziness. Indeed, Abner could see that Tawb was flabby and out of shape from the **sedentary** life he led down in his burrow.

While old Tawb moved slowly along the ground, Abner observed a small gray mouse heading toward the tricky old serpent. The snake saw the little **rodent,** too. He stopped moving and lay very still in the grass. As the mouse made his way along the forest trail, unaware of what was waiting for him, Tawb slithered into view.

"Hello, little mouse," hissed the old snake, in what he hoped was a friendly voice. "I have a **proposition** for you."

The mouse trembled as he replied, "What is it, Mr. Snake?"

"I am hungry, little mouse, and if you don't bring me the egg of a bird, I am going to eat you!" Tawb attempted a smile, but the effort only made his features more frightening.

Reading • EMC 4533 • ©2005 by Evan-Moor Corp.

Shaking from his whiskers to the tip of his tail, the little mouse managed to **stammer** his agreement. "Where shall I bring the egg when I find one?" he asked.

"I live in a hole next to the big oak tree," whispered Tawb. "I will be waiting there for you to bring me an egg. If you don't show up, I shall find you and eat you. And I will eat all of the mice in the forest as well. So mind well and do not fail."

Terrified, the little mouse went straightaway to find an egg. Soon he could be seen struggling down the path where he had met Old Tawb. He grunted as he hauled a pale blue robin's egg toward the old oak tree. The weight of the egg was heavy for his little body, and he was exhausted as he approached the hole.

"Mr. Snake," called the mouse. "I have kept my promise. Here is your egg."

"Bring it to me," hissed Tawb, "and then you may go on your way."

Screwing up all his courage, the mouse pushed the egg into the dim entryway. Tawb was waiting with his mouth opened wide. In the darkness, the poor mouse stumbled into the trap. The egg and he went down in one gulp.

The next day, Abner could see from his perch in the oak tree that the snake was very well pleased with his little trick. The satisfaction on Tawb's face was **evident** as he emerged from his hole. He was clearly delighted at having

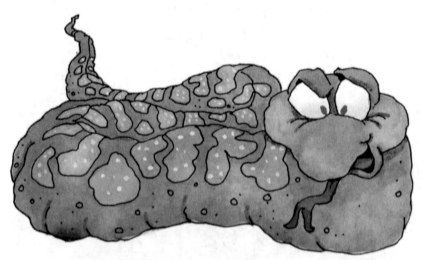

fooled the **hapless** mouse.

"**Clever** me," hissed Tawb in obvious glee. "I tricked that silly mouse into walking right into my mouth. And I made him bring me an egg in the **bargain**! Clever, clever me!"

Abner had no doubt at all that Tawb intended to try his trick again. Indeed, before an hour had passed, a chubby gray mouse came scurrying down the forest path. Just as he had done before, Tawb grew still in the tall grass and waited. And just as he had done before, Tawb **waylaid** the mouse.

"Bring me an egg, or I will eat you," said the snake. "And heed my words. If you fail, I shall eat you and all the mice in the forest as well!"

Away went the mouse on his fateful errand. Abner, watching from his perch, decided to take action. Thinking quickly, he came up with a plan. He flew to the riverbank to fetch a small stone. He found a pebble that was just the size and shape of a bird's egg. Picking it up in his beak, he zoomed quickly back to the oak tree. He wanted to be sure that he got back to Tawb's den before the mouse returned.

Within minutes, Abner saw the mouse approaching, stumbling slowly along the path pushing a **speckled** egg in front of him. Abner wasted no time.

Quickly, he **intercepted** the mouse and told him to run for his life. Then, he swooped gently to the ground and crept **stealthily** to the snake's hole.

"Mr. Snake, I've got your egg," said Abner, speaking in his best mouse voice.

"Bring it down the hole to me, and then you may go on your way," hissed Tawb. He opened his mouth wide in **anticipation** of a great feast. Abner waited a few seconds, just long enough to be sure that Tawb had opened his jaws nice and wide. Then, he dropped the pebble.

 Reading • EMC 4533 • ©2005 by Evan-Moor Corp.

Tawb knew immediately that something was **amiss**. This egg did not have a **pleasant** taste or a slick, smooth shell. It was not followed by the wonderful **sensation** of soft fur sliding down his **gullet**. Instead, this was a **harsh** and painful meal to swallow. It seemed to grate at him all the way down his esophagus. Just as he was beginning to realize that something was terribly wrong indeed, Tawb heard a voice just outside his burrow's entrance.

"I saw what you did to that mouse yesterday, Tawb, and I didn't think it was nice."

"Why, it's that meddling crow!" thought Tawb. "What have you done to me?" cried the snake angrily.

"I have tried to teach you a lesson, Tawb," Abner explained. "Normally, I am not the type to get involved in the affairs of others. But when I see such dastardly actions as yours, I feel compelled to put a stop to them. I hope this is the last we'll see of such tricky and dishonest doings on your part. And just remember this: the next stone I drop will be a good deal bigger!"

With that, Abner flapped his strong black wings and rose gracefully to the top of the oak tree. And Tawb slithered miserably down into the deepest part of his den where he passed a long and rather uncomfortable afternoon.

Questions About
ABNER ᴛʜᴇ CROW & Tawb the Snake

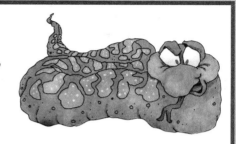

Fill in the circle that best answers each question.

1. Which characteristic was Tawb the Snake known for?
   Ⓐ his generosity
   Ⓑ his laziness
   Ⓒ his courage
   Ⓓ his energy

2. Why did Abner speak "in his best mouse voice"?
   Ⓐ So that Tawb would fall for the trick.
   Ⓑ He wanted to be sure the snake heard him.
   Ⓒ He had a pebble in his beak.
   Ⓓ The snake was hard of hearing.

3. Why was Tawb out of shape?
   Ⓐ He ate too much.
   Ⓑ He was an old snake.
   Ⓒ He didn't get any exercise.
   Ⓓ His den was comfortable.

4. Which threat did Tawb use to frighten the mice into obeying him?
   Ⓐ He said he would cut off their tails.
   Ⓑ He said he would kidnap their children.
   Ⓒ He said he would eat all the mice in the forest.
   Ⓓ He said he would eat all the animals in the forest.

5. What did Abner do in response to Tawb's trickery?
   Ⓐ He fed the snake a pebble in place of a bird's egg.
   Ⓑ He rolled a stone over the opening of Tawb's den.
   Ⓒ He warned all the mice to stay away from the area.
   Ⓓ He pecked Tawb with his strong yellow beak.

6. Abner tricked Tawb because _____.
   Ⓐ he disliked snakes
   Ⓑ the mice asked him to
   Ⓒ he enjoyed being cruel
   Ⓓ he wanted to teach Tawb a lesson

How Did They Feel?

Complete each sentence to identify the feelings of the characters in these situations. Draw a picture to illustrate each situation.

Tawb felt _____ after successfully tricking the first mouse.

The first mouse felt _____ when confronting Tawb.

Abner felt _____ as he observed Tawb's actions.

The second mouse felt _____ when Abner told him to run.

Choose the Right Meaning

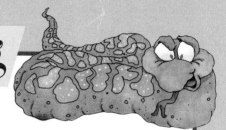

Find these highlighted words in the story. Read the sentence in which each word is found. Choose the correct meaning.

1. The word **ancient** means extremely _____.
   - Ⓐ old
   - Ⓑ pretty
   - Ⓒ worried
   - Ⓓ dangerous

2. The word **stammer** means to _____.
   - Ⓐ cough and choke
   - Ⓑ shout or speak loudly
   - Ⓒ stutter or speak haltingly
   - Ⓓ whisper or speak quietly

3. The word **evident** means _____.
   - Ⓐ strange
   - Ⓑ obvious
   - Ⓒ confusing
   - Ⓓ mysterious

4. The word **sensation** means _____.
   - Ⓐ fur
   - Ⓑ view
   - Ⓒ belief
   - Ⓓ feeling

5. The word **pleasant** means _____.
   - Ⓐ enjoyable
   - Ⓑ painful
   - Ⓒ nasty
   - Ⓓ dark

6. The word **bargain** means _____.
   - Ⓐ pen
   - Ⓑ deal
   - Ⓒ catalog
   - Ⓓ wheelbarrow

7. The word **proposition** means _____.
   - Ⓐ lie
   - Ⓑ order
   - Ⓒ proposal
   - Ⓓ demand

8. The word **intercepted** means _____.
   - Ⓐ punished
   - Ⓑ stopped on the way
   - Ⓒ sneaked up on
   - Ⓓ pretended to be interested

9. The word **stealthily** means _____.
   - Ⓐ shyly
   - Ⓑ carefully
   - Ⓒ anxiously
   - Ⓓ secretly

10. The word **gullet** means _____.
    - Ⓐ throat
    - Ⓑ tunnel
    - Ⓒ tongue
    - Ⓓ cheek

Match the Meaning

Find these **bolded** words in the story. Read the sentence
in which each word is found. Write the letter of the correct definition on the line
in front of each word.

1. _____ sedentary

2. _____ hapless

3. _____ amiss

4. _____ harsh

5. _____ speckled

6. _____ slithering

7. _____ rodent

8. _____ clever

9. _____ comfort

10. _____ waylaid

11. _____ idly

12. _____ anticipation

a. smart

b. eagerness; expectation

c. abrasive

d. gliding like a snake

e. unlucky

f. inactive

g. wrong; not as it should be

h. ambushed

i. spotted

j. class of mammal with large front teeth

k. lazily

l. ease

Where Does It Belong?

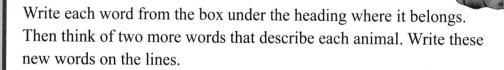

Write each word from the box under the heading where it belongs.
Then think of two more words that describe each animal. Write these
new words on the lines.

scaly   flap   furry   slither   scurry
feathery   rodent   serpent   bird

Mouse	Snake	Crow
_____	_____	_____
_____	_____	_____
_____	_____	_____
_____	_____	_____
_____	_____	_____
_____	_____	_____

A mouse and a snake are **alike** because _____

_____

A crow and a mouse are **different** because _____

_____

Reading • EMC 4533 • ©2005 by Evan-Moor Corp.

Adding *-ing* and *-ed* to Verbs

Add the suffixes **-ing** and **-ed** to each verb. You may have to drop a silent **e** or change **y** to **i**.

haul	hauling	hauled
stumble	_____	_____
exhaust	_____	_____
scurry	_____	_____
heed	_____	_____
zoom	_____	_____
intercept	_____	_____
grate	_____	_____
meddle	_____	_____
hiss	_____	_____
slither	_____	_____

Write three sentences. Use at least one word from the list in each sentence. Be sure to use all three verb forms.

_____

_____

_____

_____

Shiver & Quake

There once was a boy who lived with his father and mother. He was a dreamy lad, good-natured and kind, but not much help to his hardworking parents. He spent his days sitting in the corner and gazing into the fire or climbing trees to their highest branches and looking out into the far horizon. He was sorry to be a **disappointment** to his loved ones, but he could not hide the fact that he was different.

One evening when the family was gathered around the table eating their supper, a black cat with glowing green eyes **bounded** in through the window, hissed strangely, and then melted out the door.

The father jumped up and shut the door. Just as quickly, the mother rushed to shut the window.

"Oh!" said the father. "That cat gave me a fright!"

"Yes," said the mother, "I have a shiver and quake in my bones!"

"What's this?" demanded the boy, who had not been at all bothered by the cat and continued to eat his supper with **gusto**. "What does it mean to shiver and quake?"

The father and mother looked sadly at one another. "Our poor boy," said the father. "He knows nothing of life and seems unable to learn. How will he ever make his way in the world?"

The boy could tell that he had caused his parents sorrow in some way, and he wanted to mend it.

"No," he said firmly. "I can learn, and I will learn. I will begin by learning how to shiver and quake."

And so he put on his jacket and slung a small pack over his shoulder and set out down the road, determined to find out how to shiver and quake with the best of them.

Reading • EMC 4533 • ©2005 by Evan-Moor Corp.

Soon enough, he saw an old man camped alongside the road. The old man had a small fire blazing, and the boy strolled right up to the fire and warmed his hands over the flames.

"Good evening, sir. I thank you for allowing me to share your warm fire."

Now the old man was a robber, but he was amazed at the **pluck** of this young man who was so obviously unafraid. And he could rightly see that the boy was poor and had nothing worth stealing in any case. Curious, he asked the boy who he was and what he was doing. Gladly, the boy gave his name and told the old man about his **mission**.

The old robber smiled in the darkness. "I think I can assist you in learning to shiver and quake," he said.

He told the boy to take the west road and walk until he saw an old house made of dark stones standing on a craggy hilltop.

"The house is haunted," whispered the robber. "There you will surely learn what it is to shiver and quake."

So the boy set off on the west road as he had been told, and he walked all the rest of the night and through the next day. Just as the sun was sinking low, the boy rounded a bend in the road and saw the house rising before him, outlined against the blood-red sky.

"Why, here it is," said the boy to himself. "I hope I shall learn how to shiver and quake here, as I have been promised!"

Cheerfully, he walked up the twisting path leading to the haunted house. Brambles and broken branches made the journey more difficult, but he paid them no mind. At last, he reached the weed-covered yard that led to the front porch of the house. He pushed open the heavy door on its rusty hinges and entered the dim hall. All was silent, dusty, and covered with cobwebs. It seemed that no one had been here for many years.

As the boy looked about in the **gloom**, he felt a cool hand touch his shoulder. He turned, but could see no one.

"Is someone here?" the boy asked easily. "Who are you?"

A voice that seemed hollow and far away answered from the darkness.

"Any man who can spend three nights in this place without running away in fear will break the spell that is cast upon this house. He shall be rewarded with three trunks of gold. But alas, though many have tried, all have failed. They shiver and quake, their hearts become **faint**, and then they flee."

"I don't know how to shiver and quake," the boy told the voice. "I will pass the test. See if I don't. Though I don't know what I shall do with three trunks of gold!"

"We shall see," said the hollow voice. Then all was silent.

"Well, that was odd," said the boy, and he set to work to make himself a bit more comfortable. The boy found an old broom and swept the heaps of old ashes out of the grate. He searched about the house grounds and gathered some pieces of wood. He made a fire in the hearth. Then he cleaned off a wooden bench and drug it near the warmth. He pulled out his pocketknife and sat whittling a stick. When that was done, he stuck a piece of bread from his bag onto the end of the stick and toasted it over the roaring flames.

"Ah, this is the life," thought the boy as he rested, dreaming into the flames.

Reading • EMC 4533 • ©2005 by Evan-Moor Corp.

Around midnight, as the boy dozed on the hard bench, there came a loud banging and clanging. The boy awoke at once and watched with interest as an enormous ogre, with chains dangling from his **massive** legs, came shuffling and **clanking** into the chamber. The ogre had wild red eyes and mossy green hair. A gigantic wooden club was grasped in his leathery fist. He made low growling sounds in his throat as he **clambered** across the stone floor.

"He means me harm," thought the boy. "But I can see that he is clumsy and slow. I know just how to fix him."

So the boy got up from his bench and stood with his back toward the wide fireplace.

"Come on, ogre," he said pleasantly. "Come and get me."

The ogre shuffled forward, swinging the heavy club **awkwardly** about his head. Just as the ogre was about to bring the club down in a mighty blow, the boy jumped nimbly aside. The momentum of his swing carried the ogre into the fireplace, club and all. The ogre screamed and disappeared in a puff of acrid blue smoke. The club itself burned on through the night. The boy settled back on his bench and watched the bright blaze until his eyes grew heavy and he fell asleep.

The next day passed quietly, and again night fell. Again the boy sat upon the bench, warming himself and toasting his bread. Suddenly, from the dark nooks and corners of the room, an army of tiny goblins emerged. Their voices were joined together in a **chorus** of **shrill** shrieks. The boy simply pulled some bits of rag from his pockets and stuffed his ears so that he could not hear the **irksome** noise. Then he continued to **munch** happily on his bread.

This **infuriated** the goblins, who began to **shriek** more loudly. They ran up to the boy and began to pinch and poke at his legs with their sharp little fingers and claws.

"Enough of this," thought the boy. He picked up the broom that was sitting nearby and quickly swept the **pesky** goblins into the fire where they popped like popcorn. Tired from his efforts, the boy retired to his bench where he slept soundly by the warm fire for the rest of the night.

Reading • EMC 4533 • ©2005 by Evan-Moor Corp.

The next day passed quietly, and again night fell. "I wonder if I shall learn to shiver and quake tonight," said the boy to himself.

As darkness fell and he ate his bread by the crackling hearth, he heard a loud thumping on the front door.

"Come in!" he yelled.

A ghoul came cackling into the room, a fiendish-looking creature with black, empty eyes. He carried a black bag over his shoulder, from which he drew a set of ninepins. The pins were made of large white bones, and the balls were made of human skulls.

The ghoul peered over his shoulder at the boy, who was watching with interest.

"Would you like to play?" **wheezed** the ghoul in a **raspy** whisper.

"Why, yes, thank you," said the boy. "It has been quite dull here with nothing much to do. I would love to play a game to pass the time."

So they played for hours and hours, and the boy thought it quite good fun. As dawn's first gray light crept into the sky, the ghoul packed away his toys and slithered out the front door. And the boy stretched out on his bench and slept until the sun was bright in the sky and the birds were singing merrily.

When the boy at last opened his eyes, he sat up in astonishment. Everything seemed new and different. Instead of resting on a hard bench, he found himself in a snug bed covered with a warm quilt. Gone were the dust and cobwebs. Sun streamed through sparkling windows.

The boy leapt from his bed and ran outside. The walls of the house rose straight and strong above his head. Fruit trees bloomed in the yard, and a crystal stream burbled down the hill.

"Oh, my," said the boy aloud. "What has come to pass here?"

Immediately, the hollow voice spoke near his ear. "You have broken the spell," laughed the voice. "And now you will have your reward."

Three trunks of gold suddenly appeared at the boy's feet. He looked at the bright coins for a moment or two, then tightly closed the trunks and stacked them in the cellar. He spent the day climbing trees, listening to the birds, and watching fleecy clouds sail across a bright blue sky.

After a few such jolly days had passed, the boy stuffed his bag with gold coins and set off for his parents' home.

When he came whistling up the walk, his parents rushed out to meet him.

"Oh, my son," cried his mother, "it is so good to see you! Have you learned to shiver and quake?"

"No, Mother, but I have found my way in the world. Look at this!" And he opened the bag and spilled the gold coins into the hands of his astonished parents.

And so it turned out that the boy never did learn to shiver and quake, but he did learn that courage brings a happy life, and so he thought no more about it.

Reading • EMC 4533 • ©2005 by Evan-Moor Corp.

Questions About
Shiver & Quake

Fill in the circle that best answers each question.

1. The boy felt bad because he _____.
   Ⓐ had no money
   Ⓑ didn't want to work
   Ⓒ spent all his time daydreaming
   Ⓓ caused his parents to worry

2. The robber did not try to steal from the boy because he _____.
   Ⓐ wanted the boy to go to the haunted house
   Ⓑ could tell that the boy had no possessions
   Ⓒ was afraid of the boy
   Ⓓ liked the boy

3. The boy stuffed his ears with rags because the _____.
   Ⓐ ghoul wheezed too loudly
   Ⓑ ogre's roars hurt his ears
   Ⓒ sizzle of the fire kept him awake
   Ⓓ goblins' shrieks were so annoying

4. On the third morning, the boy awoke to find _____.
   Ⓐ the house and its surroundings were now lovely
   Ⓑ all the spooky creatures had returned
   Ⓒ his bread had been eaten by mice
   Ⓓ the hollow voice laughing at him

5. What caused the spell on the house to be broken?
   Ⓐ the boy's lack of fear
   Ⓑ the creatures burned up
   Ⓒ the robber cast a new spell
   Ⓓ the time of the spell was up

6. What did the boy do with the trunks of gold?
   Ⓐ He put them under the bed.
   Ⓑ He stacked them in the cellar.
   Ⓒ He buried them in the garden.
   Ⓓ He took them to his parents.

Write About the Story

Some people might say the boy in this story was silly and not very bright. Others might disagree with this statement. What do you think? Defend your position with events from the story.

_____

_____

_____

_____

_____

_____

_____

_____

_____

_____

_____

_____

Choose the Right Meaning

Find these highlighted words in the story. Read the sentence in which each word is found. Choose the correct meaning.

1. Which of these would be a **disappointment**?
   - Ⓐ new toys
   - Ⓑ a surprise party
   - Ⓒ losing the championship
   - Ⓓ winning the state lottery

2. The word **gusto** in this story means _____.
   - Ⓐ enthusiasm and enjoyment
   - Ⓑ sadness and longing
   - Ⓒ pain and suffering
   - Ⓓ fear and dread

3. The word **pluck** in this story means _____.
   - Ⓐ fancy clothes
   - Ⓑ confidence
   - Ⓒ wealth
   - Ⓓ voice

4. The word **shrill** describes a sound that is _____.
   - Ⓐ soft and melodic
   - Ⓑ deep and rumbling
   - Ⓒ muffled and rhythmic
   - Ⓓ high-pitched and piercing

5. The word **awkwardly** means about the same as _____.
   - Ⓐ gracefully
   - Ⓑ clumsily
   - Ⓒ nimbly
   - Ⓓ quickly

6. Which of these could <u>not</u> be described as **massive**?
   - Ⓐ a twig
   - Ⓑ a boulder
   - Ⓒ a tree trunk
   - Ⓓ an elephant

7. When might you **shriek with delight**?
   - Ⓐ when you see a scary movie
   - Ⓑ when you stub your toe
   - Ⓒ when you get a new bicycle
   - Ⓓ when a friend jumps out and says "boo"

8. A house that is **gloomy** is _____.
   - Ⓐ friendly looking
   - Ⓑ brightly lit
   - Ⓒ dark
   - Ⓓ old

9. Which word is a synonym for **bounded**?
   - Ⓐ sat down
   - Ⓑ tied up
   - Ⓒ ran off
   - Ⓓ jumped

10. How would you move if you **clambered** up the stairs?
    - Ⓐ clumsily
    - Ⓑ on tiptoe
    - Ⓒ one step at a time
    - Ⓓ by leaps and bounds

Which Word Fits?

Complete each sentence using a word from the box. If you need help with the meaning of the words, look for them in the story and read the sentences in which they are found.

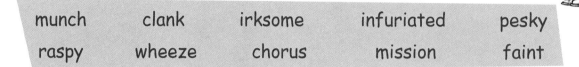

munch	clank	irksome	infuriated	pesky
raspy	wheeze	chorus	mission	faint

1. When we went shopping, our _____ was to find the perfect birthday gift for Jenny.

2. Dad was _____ when Roger and I spilled paint on the garage floor.

3. The _____ crows kept eating the seeds that Uncle John planted in his garden.

4. My baby sister is _____ when she chews on my homework.

5. The anchor dropped on the ship's deck with a loud _____.

6. Maria talked on the phone until her voice became _____.

7. Lydia was happy when she was chosen to sing in the _____.

8. I like to _____ on potato chips or popcorn while I watch TV.

9. Mr. Wilson knew that he had only a _____ chance to win the election, but he never stopped trying.

10. Asthma sometimes causes people to _____.

True or False?

The statements below are false. Change one word in each statement to make it true and then rewrite the statement.

1. The boy's parents were worried about him because he was so fearful.

_____

_____

2. The ogre had blue hair and carried a large club in his fist.

_____

_____

3. The goblins poked the boy with their sharp little sticks.

_____

_____

4. The ghoul carried a black box over his shoulder.

_____

_____

5. When the boy awoke after the first night, he found himself in a comfortable bed.

_____

_____

6. The boy learned that courage could help him live a miserable life.

_____

_____

Before and After

Fill in each blank with **before** or **after**.

1. The boy left home _____ the cat came into the house.

2. The ogre attacked the boy _____ the goblins appeared.

3. The boy was given three trunks of gold _____ he met the robber.

4. The robber told the boy about the haunted house _____ the boy left home.

5. The boy and the ghoul played ninepins _____ the ogre attacked the boy.

6. The boy took a bagful of gold coins to his parents _____ he went to the haunted house.

7. The boy put the trunks of gold in the cellar _____ he played ninepins with the ghoul.

8. The boy put on his jacket _____ he left home.

9. The boy stuffed his ears with rags _____ the goblins began to pinch him.

10. The boy built a fire in the fireplace _____ he whittled a stick.

Tracking Form

Topic	Color in each page you complete.					
Beauty and the Beast	10	11	12	13	14	15
Tracking Tornadoes	20	21	22	23	24	25
The Midas Touch: A Greek Myth	30	31	32	33	34	35
Otzi the Iceman	41	42	43	44	45	46
The Tiger and the Jackals	52	53	54	55	56	57
Silkworms	62	63	64	65	66	67
Joy Adamson: Living with Lions	72	73	74	75	76	77
Old Bragwynn the Pirate	84	85	86	87	88	89
Kangaroo Almanac	95	96	97	98	99	100
How Shalbus Egbert Bested the Bear	106	107	108	109	110	111
Abner the Crow and Tawb the Snake	116	117	118	119	120	121
Shiver and Quake	129	130	131	132	133	134

Page 10

Skills: Reading Story Details; Making Inferences

Questions About Beauty and the Beast

Fill in the circle that best answers each question.

1. Beauty asked her father to bring her _____
   Ⓐ a chrysanthemum
   Ⓑ a dandelion
   Ⓒ a daisy
   ● a rose

2. Beauty's sisters were _____
   Ⓐ kind and generous
   ● grumpy and selfish
   Ⓒ caring and obedient
   Ⓓ thoughtful and hardworking

3. Beauty went to live with the Beast because _____
   Ⓐ she wanted to live in a palace
   ● she wanted to help her father
   Ⓒ she was kidnapped
   Ⓓ he was hungry

4. It seemed to Beauty that the Beast often felt _____
   Ⓐ happy
   Ⓑ angry
   Ⓒ silly
   ● sad

5. The Beast allowed Beauty to leave him because _____
   ● her father was very ill
   Ⓑ she wanted to attend school
   Ⓒ she needed to go shopping
   Ⓓ she wanted to celebrate her birthday with her family

6. At the end of the story, the Beast said that he had been enchanted by _____
   Ⓐ an evil fairy
   ● an old sorcerer
   Ⓒ a wicked goblin
   Ⓓ a cruel magician

Page 11
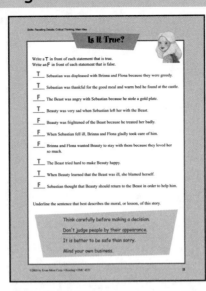

Skills: Reading Details; Critical Thinking; Main Idea

Is It True?

Write a T in front of each statement that is true.
Write an F in front of each statement that is false.

T Sebastian was displeased with Brinna and Flona because they were greedy.

T Sebastian was thankful for the good meal and warm bed he found at the castle.

F The Beast was angry with Sebastian because he stole a gold plate.

T Beauty was very sad when Sebastian left her with the Beast.

F Beauty was frightened of the Beast because he treated her badly.

F When Sebastian fell ill, Brinna and Flona gladly took care of him.

F Brinna and Flona wanted Beauty to stay with them because they loved her so much.

T The Beast tried hard to make Beauty happy.

T When Beauty learned that the Beast was ill, she blamed herself.

F Sebastian thought that Beauty should return to the Beast in order to help him.

Underline the sentence that best describes the moral, or lesson, of this story.

Think carefully before making a decision.
Don't judge people by their appearance.
It is better to be safe than sorry.
Mind your own business.

Page 12
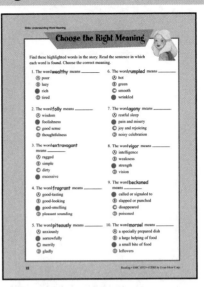

Skills: Understanding Word Meaning

Choose the Right Meaning

Find these highlighted words in the story. Read the sentence in which each word is found. Choose the correct meaning.

1. The word **wealthy** means _____
   Ⓐ poor
   Ⓑ lazy
   ● rich
   Ⓓ tired

2. The word **folly** means _____
   Ⓐ wisdom
   ● foolishness
   Ⓒ good sense
   Ⓓ thoughtfulness

3. The word **extravagant** means _____
   Ⓐ ragged
   Ⓑ simple
   Ⓒ dirty
   ● excessive

4. The word **fragrant** means _____
   Ⓐ good-tasting
   Ⓑ good-looking
   ● good-smelling
   Ⓓ pleasant sounding

5. The word **piteously** means _____
   Ⓐ anxiously
   ● sorrowfully
   Ⓒ merrily
   Ⓓ gladly

6. The word **rumpled** means _____
   Ⓐ hot
   Ⓑ green
   Ⓒ smooth
   ● wrinkled

7. The word **agony** means _____
   Ⓐ restful sleep
   ● pain and misery
   Ⓒ joy and rejoicing
   Ⓓ noisy celebration

8. The word **vigor** means _____
   Ⓐ intelligence
   Ⓑ weakness
   ● strength
   Ⓓ vision

9. The word **beckoned** means _____
   ● called or signaled to
   Ⓑ slapped or punched
   Ⓒ disappeared
   Ⓓ poisoned

10. The word **morsel** means _____
   Ⓐ a specially prepared dish
   Ⓑ a large helping of food
   ● a small bite of food
   Ⓓ leftovers

Page 13

Skills: Understanding Word Meaning; Using Vocabulary in Context

Draw and Write

Draw a picture to illustrate the meaning of each word. Look back at the story to help you.

goblet | soiled
frock | tapestries

Write sentences using all four words.
Answers will vary, but should include all four words used correctly.

Page 14
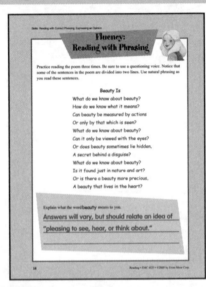

Skills: Reading with Correct Phrasing; Expressing an Opinion

Fluency: Reading with Phrasing

Practice reading the poem three times. Be sure to use a questioning voice. Notice that some of the sentences in the poem are divided into two lines. Use natural phrasing as you read these sentences.

Beauty Is

What do we know about beauty?
How do we know what it means?
Can beauty be measured by actions
Or only by that which is seen?
What do we know about beauty?
Can it only be viewed with the eyes?
Or does beauty sometimes lie hidden,
A secret behind a disguise?
What do we know about beauty?
Is it found just in nature and art?
Or is there a beauty more precious,
A beauty that lives in the heart?

Explain what the word **beauty** means to you.
Answers will vary, but should relate an idea of "pleasing to see, hear, or think about."

Page 15
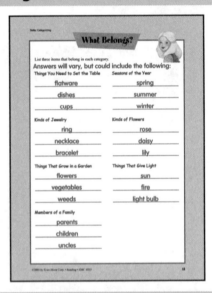

Skills: Categorizing

What Belongs?

List three items that belong in each category.
Answers will vary, but could include the following:

Things You Need to Set the Table
flatware
dishes
cups

Seasons of the Year
spring
summer
winter

Kinds of Jewelry
ring
necklace
bracelet

Kinds of Flowers
rose
daisy
lily

Things That Grow in a Garden
flowers
vegetables
weeds

Things That Give Light
sun
fire
light bulb

Members of a Family
parents
children
uncles

Page 20

Skills: Reading Story Details; Making Inferences

Questions About Tracking Tornadoes

Fill in the circle that best answers each question.

1. In which of these states is a tornado most likely to occur?
   Ⓐ Maine
   Ⓑ Hawaii
   Ⓒ New York
   ● Oklahoma

2. The collision of warm and cool air currents often creates _____
   ● a thunderstorm
   Ⓑ a snowstorm
   Ⓒ a frosty day
   Ⓓ a clear sky

3. The swirling winds of a tornado are shaped like _____
   Ⓐ an hourglass
   ● a funnel
   Ⓒ a spoon
   Ⓓ a tree

4. Scientists study tornadoes because they hope to _____
   ● predict when tornadoes will occur
   Ⓑ watch tornadoes destroy houses
   Ⓒ have fun in the rain
   Ⓓ see a hailstorm

5. A strong thunderstorm in which a tornado forms is called _____
   Ⓐ a powercloud
   Ⓑ a plainstm
   ● a supercell
   Ⓓ a rainbow

6. Which of the following do scientists use to gather information about storms?
   Ⓐ a helicopter
   Ⓑ a parachute
   Ⓒ a rocket
   ● a weather balloon

Page 21
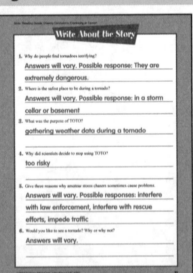

Skills: Reading Details; Drawing Conclusions; Expressing an Opinion

Write About the Story

1. Why do people find tornadoes terrifying?
   Answers will vary. Possible response: They are extremely dangerous.

2. Where is the safest place to be during a tornado?
   Answers will vary. Possible response: in a storm cellar or basement

3. What was the purpose of TOTO?
   gathering weather data during a tornado

4. Why did scientists decide to stop using TOTO?
   too risky

5. Give three reasons why amateur storm chasers sometimes cause problems.
   Answers will vary. Possible responses: interfere with law enforcement, interfere with rescue efforts, impede traffic

6. Would you like to see a tornado? Why or why not?
   Answers will vary.

Page 22

Skills: Understanding Word Meaning

Choose the Right Meaning

Find these highlighted words in the story. Read the sentence in which each word is found. Choose the correct meaning.

1. A **siren** is _____
   ● a loud alarm or danger signal
   Ⓑ a printed announcement
   Ⓒ a newspaper
   Ⓓ a clock

2. **Humidity** is the _____
   Ⓐ speed of the wind
   Ⓑ temperature at ground level
   ● amount of moisture in the air
   Ⓓ amount of snowfall in a given year

3. Which of the following is a kind of **instrument**?
   Ⓐ a scientist
   Ⓑ a tornado
   Ⓒ a state
   ● a thermometer

4. The word **recklessly** means about the same as _____
   Ⓐ carefully
   ● carelessly
   Ⓒ cautiously
   Ⓓ thoughtfully

5. In this story, the word **storage** means _____
   ● a place to keep things that are safe
   Ⓑ a place to bury things
   Ⓒ a place to buy things
   Ⓓ a place to live

6. A **dramatic** event is one that is _____
   Ⓐ funny and comical
   Ⓑ dull and uninteresting
   Ⓒ common and ordinary
   ● spectacular and theatrical

7. Which of the following is an antonym for **amateurs**?
   Ⓐ beginners
   Ⓑ novices
   ● professionals
   Ⓓ trainees

8. Which of the following is not a meaning for **method**?
   ● role
   Ⓑ process
   Ⓒ technique
   Ⓓ procedure

9. Something that is **fascinating** is _____
   Ⓐ boring
   Ⓑ bright
   Ⓒ difficult
   ● interesting

10. An **observatory** is used to _____
   Ⓐ cook things
   ● study things
   Ⓒ store things
   Ⓓ paint things

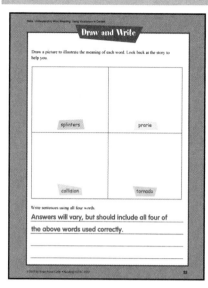

Draw and Write

Draw a picture to illustrate the meaning of each word. Look back at the story to help you.

splinters	prarie
collision	tornado

Write sentences using all four words.

Answers will vary, but should include all four of the above words used correctly.

Fact or Opinion?

A fact tells information that is true.
An opinion tells about someone's thoughts or feelings.

Write fact or opinion after each statement.

1. Tornadoes are very powerful storms. — fact
2. Tornadoes form within supercells. — fact
3. It would be fun to be a tornado tracker. — opinion
4. People should not live in places where tornadoes occur. — opinion
5. Scientists who study tornadoes are foolish. — opinion
6. Tornadoes are exciting and interesting. — opinion
7. Most tornadoes take place in spring and early summer. — fact
8. A storm cellar is a good place to go during a tornado. — fact

Write two or three sentences telling how you might feel and what you might do if you saw a tornado approaching your house.

Answers will vary.

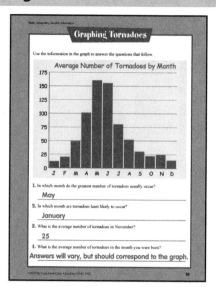

Graphing Tornadoes

Use the information in the graph to answer the questions that follow.

Average Number of Tornadoes by Month

1. In which month do the greatest number of tornadoes usually occur?
   May
2. In which month are tornadoes least likely to occur?
   January
3. What is the average number of tornadoes in November?
   25
4. What is the average number of tornadoes in the month you were born?
   Answers will vary, but should correspond to the graph.

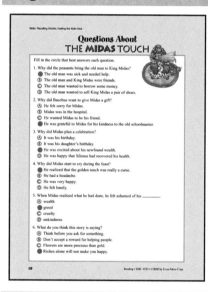

Questions About THE MIDAS TOUCH

Fill in the circle that best answers each question.

1. Why did the peasants bring the old man to King Midas?
   - The old man was sick and needed help.
   - ● The old man and King Midas were friends.
   - The old man wanted to borrow some money.
   - The old man wanted to sell King Midas a pair of shoes.

2. Why did Bacchus want to give Midas a gift?
   - He felt sorry for Midas.
   - Midas was in the hospital.
   - He wanted Midas to be his friend.
   - ● He was grateful to Midas for his kindness to the old schoolmaster.

3. Why did Midas plan a celebration?
   - It was his birthday.
   - It was his daughter's birthday.
   - He was excited about his newfound wealth.
   - ● He was happy that Silenus had recovered his health.

4. Why did Midas start to cry during the feast?
   - ● He realized that the golden touch was really a curse.
   - He had a headache.
   - He was very happy.
   - He felt lonely.

5. When Midas realized what he had done, he felt ashamed of his _____
   - wealth
   - ● greed
   - cruelty
   - unkindness

6. What do you think this story is saying?
   - ● Think before you ask for something.
   - Don't accept a reward for helping people.
   - Flowers are more precious than gold.
   - Riches alone will not make you happy.

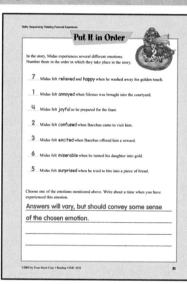

Put It in Order

In the story, Midas experiences several different emotions. Number them in the order in which they take place in the story.

7 Midas felt relieved and happy when he washed away his golden touch.

1 Midas felt annoyed when Silenus was brought into the courtyard.

4 Midas felt joyful as he prepared for the feast.

2 Midas felt confused when Bacchus came to visit him.

3 Midas felt excited when Bacchus offered him a reward.

6 Midas felt miserable when he turned his daughter into gold.

5 Midas felt surprised when he tried to bite into a piece of bread.

Choose one of the emotions mentioned above. Write about a time when you have experienced this emotion.

Answers will vary, but should convey some sense of the chosen emotion.

Choose the Right Meaning

Find these highlighted words in the story. Read the sentence in which each word is found. Choose the correct meaning.

1. The word jostled means _____
   - played a game
   - tripped and fell
   - sat straight and tall
   - ● bumped and pushed

2. The word nugget means _____
   - ● a small lump
   - a plank
   - a book
   - a frog

3. The word recover means _____
   - to get smaller
   - to get bigger
   - ● to get better
   - to be sad

4. The word replica means _____
   - a beautiful flower
   - ● an exact copy
   - a wool coat
   - an old book

5. The word plunged means _____
   - leaped or flew over
   - ● jumped or dived in
   - read carefully
   - took a nap

6. The word transformed means _____
   - explained
   - smashed
   - ● changed
   - painted

7. The word doubtful means _____
   - ● uncertain
   - unkind
   - unhappy
   - unfeeling

8. The word mercy means _____
   - cruel laughter
   - revenge and anger
   - misery and sadness
   - ● kindness and pity

9. The word ruckus means _____
   - celebration
   - ● commotion
   - backpack
   - ball game

10. The word opportunity means _____
    - ● chance
    - job
    - time
    - permission

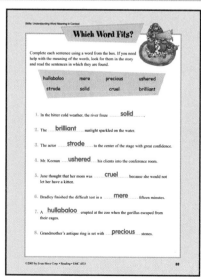

Which Word Fits?

Complete each sentence using a word from the box. If you need help with the meaning of the words, look for them in the story and read the sentences in which they are found.

hullabaloo	mere	precious	ushered
strode	solid	cruel	brilliant

1. In the bitter cold weather, the river froze solid
2. The brilliant sunlight sparkled on the water.
3. The actor strode to the center of the stage with great confidence.
4. Mr. Keenan ushered his clients into the conference room.
5. Jane thought that her mom was cruel because she would not let her have a kitten.
6. Bradley finished the difficult test in a mere fifteen minutes.
7. A hullabaloo erupted at the zoo when the gorillas escaped from their cages.
8. Grandmother's antique ring is set with precious stones.

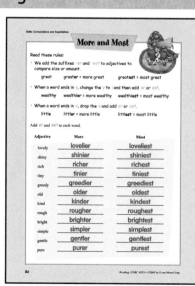

More and Most

Read these rules:

- We add the suffixes -er and -est to adjectives to compare size or amount.
  great   greater = more great   greatest = most great
- When a word ends in y, change the y to i and then add er or est.
  wealthy   wealthier = more wealthy   wealthiest = most wealthy
- When a word ends in e, drop the e and add er or est.
  little   littler = more little   littlest = most little

Add er and est to each word.

Adjective	More	Most
lovely	lovelier	loveliest
shiny	shinier	shiniest
rich	richer	richest
tiny	tinier	tiniest
greedy	greedier	greediest
old	older	oldest
kind	kinder	kindest
rough	rougher	roughest
bright	brighter	brightest
simple	simpler	simplest
gentle	gentler	gentlest
pure	purer	purest

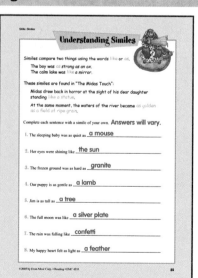

Understanding Similes

Similes compare two things using the words like or as.
The boy was as strong as an ox.
The calm lake was like a mirror.

These similes are found in "The Midas Touch":
Midas drew back in horror at the sight of his dear daughter standing like a statue.
At the same moment, the waters of the river became as golden as a field of ripe grain.

Complete each sentence with a simile of your own. Answers will vary.

1. The sleeping baby was as quiet as a mouse
2. Her eyes were shining like the sun
3. The frozen ground was as hard as granite
4. Our puppy is as gentle as a lamb
5. Jim is as tall as a tree
6. The full moon was like a silver plate
7. The rain was falling like confetti
8. My happy heart felt as light as a feather

Questions About Otzi the Iceman

Fill in the circle that best answers each question.

1. How was Otzi found?
- Ⓐ A camper's dog dug him up.
- Ⓑ He washed up on the shore of a lake.
- ● Hikers saw his skull sticking out of the ice.
- Ⓓ He was uncovered by a landslide.

2. Why was this discovery called the "Iceman"?
- Ⓐ The body was very cold.
- ● The body had been buried in ice.
- Ⓒ He lived during the Ice Age.
- Ⓓ He had to be refrigerated to preserve him.

3. Scientists believe Otzi lived about ____.
- Ⓐ 500 years ago
- Ⓑ 1,000 years ago
- Ⓒ 2,000 years ago
- ● 5,000 years ago

4. Otzi probably died of injuries he received ____.
- ● in a fall
- Ⓑ in a fight
- Ⓒ from a bear
- Ⓓ while making a fire

5. No one found Otzi for many years because has was ____.
- Ⓐ covered with sand
- Ⓑ hidden in deep woods
- ● buried in the snow and ice
- Ⓓ at the bottom a deep lake

6. Which of these statements about Otzi is true?
- ● Otzi is the oldest human body ever found.
- Ⓑ Otzi was found in Germany.
- Ⓒ Otzi was female.
- Ⓓ Otzi had a gun.

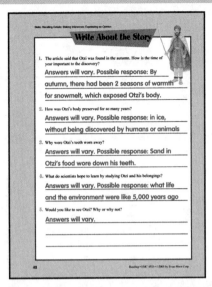

Write About the Story

1. The article said that Otzi was found in the autumn. How is the time of year important to the discovery?
Answers will vary. Possible response: By autumn, there had been 2 seasons of warmth for snowmelt, which exposed Otzi's body.

2. How was Otzi's body preserved for so many years?
Answers will vary. Possible response: in ice, without being discovered by humans or animals

3. Why were Otzi's teeth worn away?
Answers will vary. Possible response: Sand in Otzi's food wore down his teeth.

4. What do scientists hope to learn by studying Otzi and his belongings?
Answers will vary. Possible response: what life and the environment were like 5,000 years ago

5. Would you like to see Otzi? Why or why not?
Answers will vary.

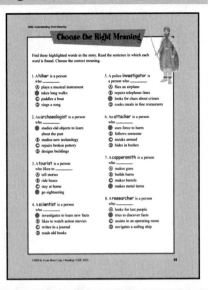

Choose the Right Meaning

Find these highlighted words in the story. Read the sentence in which each word is found. Choose the correct meaning.

1. A **hiker** is a person who ____
- Ⓐ plays a musical instrument
- ● takes long walks
- Ⓒ paddles a boat
- Ⓓ sings a song

2. An **archaeologist** is a person who ____
- ● studies old objects to learn about the past
- Ⓑ studies new technology
- Ⓒ repairs broken pottery
- Ⓓ designs buildings

3. A **tourist** is a person who likes to ____
- Ⓐ tell stories
- Ⓑ ride buses
- Ⓒ stay at home
- ● go sightseeing

4. A **scientist** is a person who ____
- ● investigates to learn new facts
- Ⓑ likes to watch action movies
- Ⓒ writes in a journal
- Ⓓ reads old books

5. A police **investigator** is a person who ____
- Ⓐ flies an airplane
- Ⓑ repairs telephone lines
- ● looks for clues about crimes
- Ⓓ cooks meals in fine restaurants

6. An **attacker** is a person who ____
- ● uses force to harm
- Ⓑ follows someone
- Ⓒ sneaks around
- Ⓓ hides in bushes

7. A **coppersmith** is a person who ____
- Ⓐ makes guns
- Ⓑ builds barns
- Ⓒ makes barrels
- ● makes metal items

8. A **researcher** is a person who ____
- Ⓐ looks for lost people
- ● tries to discover facts
- Ⓒ assists in an operating room
- Ⓓ navigates a sailing ship

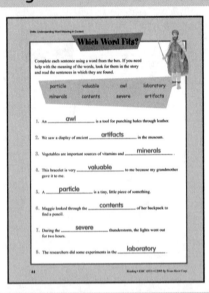

Which Word Fits?

Complete each sentence using a word from the box. If you need help with the meaning of the words, look for them in the story and read the sentences in which they are found.

particle   valuable   awl   laboratory
minerals   contents   severe   artifacts

1. An **awl** is a tool for punching holes through leather.
2. We saw a display of ancient **artifacts** in the museum.
3. Vegetables are important sources of vitamins and **minerals**.
4. This bracelet is very **valuable** to me because my grandmother gave it to me.
5. A **particle** is a tiny, little piece of something.
6. Maggie looked through the **contents** of her backpack to find a pencil.
7. During the **severe** thunderstorm, the lights went out for two hours.
8. The researchers did some experiments in the **laboratory**.

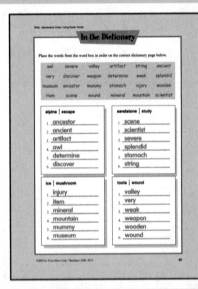

In the Dictionary

Place the words from the word box in order on the correct dictionary page below.

owl   severe   valley   artifact   string   ancient
very   discover   weapon   determine   weak   splendid
museum   ancestor   mummy   stomach   injury   wooden
item   scene   wound   mineral   mountain   scientist

alpine | escape
1. ancestor
2. ancient
3. artifact
4. awl
5. determine
6. discover

sandstone | study
1. scene
2. scientist
3. severe
4. splendid
5. stomach
6. string

ice | mushroom
1. injury
2. item
3. mineral
4. mountain
5. mummy
6. museum

tools | wound
1. valley
2. very
3. weak
4. weapon
5. wooden
6. wound

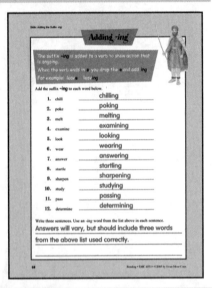

Adding -ing

The suffix **-ing** is added to a verb to show action that is ongoing.
When the verb ends in **e** you drop the **e** and adding. For example: leave → leaving

Add the suffix -ing to each word below.

1. chill   chilling
2. poke   poking
3. melt   melting
4. examine   examining
5. look   looking
6. wear   wearing
7. answer   answering
8. startle   startling
9. sharpen   sharpening
10. study   studying
11. pass   passing
12. determine   determining

Write three sentences. Use an -ing word from the list above in each sentence.
Answers will vary, but should include three words from the above list used correctly.

Questions About THE TIGER AND THE JACKALS

Fill in the circle that best answers each question.

1. The tiger normally got his food by ____.
- Ⓐ chasing it until he caught it
- Ⓑ waiting for people to bring it to him
- Ⓒ catching his prey while they were sleeping
- ● frightening his prey so much that they could not move

2. One day, the tiger suddenly realized that ____.
- Ⓐ he had eaten all the animals in the forest
- Ⓑ the animals had found new homes
- ● he missed the other animals
- Ⓓ he had grown too fat to hunt

3. When the tiger roared at the jackals, they ____.
- Ⓐ fell on the ground in fear
- Ⓑ laughed at the tiger
- ● ran away
- Ⓓ cried

4. The jackals tricked the tiger into ____.
- Ⓐ falling into a trap
- Ⓑ leaping off a cliff
- ● jumping into a well
- Ⓓ tumbling into a pool of quicksand

5. Devak warned Mita to be careful in the forest because ____.
- Ⓐ the little animals had come back
- Ⓑ there could be a tiger in the forest
- ● there could be a jackal in the forest
- Ⓓ there could be an elephant in the forest

6. Why did Devak bring Mita into the forest to tell her this story?
- Ⓐ Because it was too cold in the house.
- Ⓑ Because he wanted to help her hunt for food.
- ● Because he hoped they would see a rabbit in the forest.
- Ⓓ Because his father had told him the story in the forest.

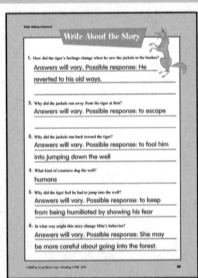

Write About the Story

1. How did the tiger's feelings change when he saw the jackals in the bushes?
Answers will vary. Possible response: He reverted to his old ways.

2. Why did the jackals run away from the tiger at first?
Answers will vary. Possible response: to escape

3. Why did the jackals run back toward the tiger?
Answers will vary. Possible response: to fool him into jumping down the well

4. What kind of creatures dug the well?
humans

5. Why did the tiger feel he had to jump into the well?
Answers will vary. Possible response: to keep from being humiliated by showing his fear

6. In what way might this story change Mita's behavior?
Answers will vary. Possible response: She may be more careful about going into the forest.

Choose the Right Meaning

Find these highlighted words in the story. Read the sentence in which each word is found. Choose the correct meaning.

1. The word **lolling** means ____
- Ⓐ bucking brutally
- ● lounging lazily
- Ⓒ jumping jerkily
- Ⓓ sitting sadly

2. The word **cowering** means ____
- Ⓐ calling out
- Ⓑ cooking
- ● cringing
- Ⓓ crying

3. The word **mangy** means ____
- ● scruffy
- Ⓑ sleek
- Ⓒ fluffy
- Ⓓ blue

4. The word **insolence** means ____
- ● rudeness
- Ⓑ joyfulness
- Ⓒ happiness
- Ⓓ sleepiness

5. The word **bolted** means ____
- Ⓐ went to sleep
- Ⓑ swallowed
- ● ran away quickly
- Ⓓ hid

6. The word **brashness** means ____
- Ⓐ grumpiness
- ● boldness and foolhardiness
- Ⓒ sweetness and gentleness
- Ⓓ shyness and bashfulness

7. The word **entranced** means ____
- Ⓐ worried
- Ⓑ excited
- Ⓒ annoyed
- ● spellbound

8. The word **devour** means to ____
- Ⓐ tie up
- ● eat hungrily
- Ⓒ scold angrily
- Ⓓ sneak up on

9. The phrase **to lose face** means to ____
- Ⓐ hide from view
- Ⓑ turn the other way
- ● look undignified
- Ⓓ cover up the face

10. The word **pursue** means to ____
- Ⓐ ask for help
- Ⓑ look high and low
- Ⓒ read carefully
- ● chase after

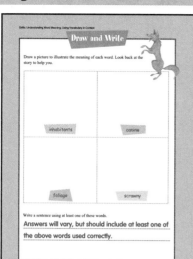

Page 55 — Draw and Write

Draw a picture to illustrate the meaning of each word. Look back at the story to help you.

inhabitants — canine
foliage — scrawny

Write a sentence using at least one of these words.

Answers will vary, but should include at least one of the above words used correctly.

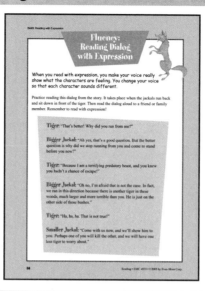

Page 56 — Fluency: Reading Dialog with Expression

When you read with expression, you make your voice really show what the characters are feeling. You change your voice so that each character sounds different.

Practice reading this dialog from the story. It takes place when the jackals run back and sit down in front of the tiger. Then read the dialog aloud to a friend or family member. Remember to read with expression!

Tiger: "That's better! Why did you run from me?"

Bigger Jackal: "Ah yes, that's a good question. But the better question is why did we stop running from you and come to stand before you now?"

Tiger: "Because I am a terrifying predatory beast, and you knew you hadn't a chance of escape!"

Bigger Jackal: "Oh no, I'm afraid that is not the case. In fact, we ran in this direction because there is another tiger in these woods, much larger and more terrible than you. He is just on the other side of those bushes."

Tiger: "Ha, ha, ha. That is not true!"

Smaller Jackal: "Come with us now, and we'll show him to you. Perhaps one of you will kill the other, and we will have one less tiger to worry about."

Page 57 — What Do You Think?

Describe your favorite part of the story.
Answers will vary.

Why did you like this part of the story best?

Draw a picture to illustrate this part of the story.

Page 62 — Questions About Silkworms

Fill in the circle that best answers each question.

1. Which of these do silkworms eat?
   Ⓐ chopped lettuce
   ● mulberry leaves
   Ⓒ seaweed
   Ⓓ milkweed

2. How many times in their lives do silkworms molt, or shed their skins?
   Ⓐ one
   Ⓑ two
   ● four
   Ⓓ three

3. Silk glands and the spinneret function to help the silkworm ____.
   Ⓐ molt for the last time
   Ⓑ change into a pupa
   Ⓒ digest its food
   ● spin its cocoon

4. If allowed to live out its life cycle, a silkworm emerges from the cocoon as ____.
   Ⓐ a grasshopper
   Ⓑ a butterfly
   Ⓒ a hornet
   ● a moth

5. When a silkworm caterpillar reaches its full size, it ____.
   ● stops eating
   Ⓑ stops moving
   Ⓒ eats more than ever
   Ⓓ dies

6. Vegetarian silk is silk that ____.
   ● is made by a process that allows the silkworms to live out their life cycle
   Ⓑ is made by feeding the silkworms vegetables
   Ⓒ vegetarians wear
   Ⓓ is made from cotton

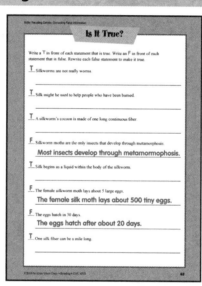

Page 63 — Is It True?

Write a T in front of each statement that is true. Write an F in front of each statement that is false. Rewrite each false statement to make it true.

T Silkworms are not really worms.

T Silk might be used to help people who have been burned.

T A silkworm's cocoon is made of one long continuous fiber.

F Silkworm moths are the only insects that develop through metamorphosis.
Most insects develop through metamormophosis.

T Silk begins as a liquid within the body of the silkworm.

F The female silkworm moth lays about 5 large eggs.
The female silk moth lays about 500 tiny eggs.

F The eggs hatch in 30 days.
The eggs hatch after about 20 days.

T One silk fiber can be a mile long.

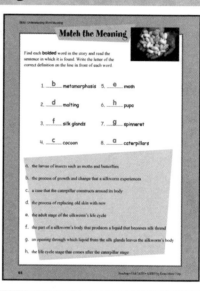

Page 64 — Match the Meaning

Find each bolded word in the story and read the sentence in which it is found. Write the letter of the correct definition on the line in front of each word.

1. b metamorphosis   5. e moth
2. d molting   6. h pupa
3. f silk glands   7. g spinneret
4. c cocoon   8. a caterpillars

a. the larvae of insects such as moths and butterflies
b. the process of growth and change that a silkworm experiences
c. a case that the caterpillar constructs around its body
d. the process of replacing old skin with new
e. the adult stage of the silkworm's life cycle
f. the part of a silkworm's body that produces a liquid that becomes silk thread
g. an opening through which liquid from the silk glands leaves the silkworm's body
h. the life cycle stage that comes after the caterpillar stage

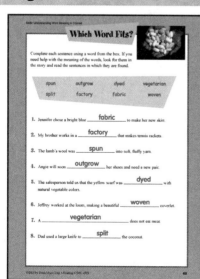

Page 65 — Which Word Fits?

Complete each sentence using a word from the box. If you need help with the meaning of the words, look for them in the story and read the sentences in which they are found.

spun   outgrow   dyed   vegetarian
split   factory   fabric   woven

1. Jennifer chose a bright blue **fabric** to make her new skirt.
2. My brother works in a **factory** that makes tennis rackets.
3. The lamb's wool was **spun** into soft, fluffy yarn.
4. Angie will soon **outgrow** her shoes and need a new pair.
5. The salesperson told us that the yellow scarf was **dyed** with natural vegetable colors.
6. Jeffrey worked at the loom, making a beautiful **woven** coverlet.
7. A **vegetarian** does not eat meat.
8. Dad used a large knife to **split** the coconut.

Page 66 — Know Your Roots

Many English words have parts that come from Greek and Latin, two ancient languages. Here are the meanings of some word parts:

ad—to   cred—believe   in—not   fac—make
fila—thread   here—stick   cycl—circular struct—build
viv—live   meta—change   morph—form, shape

Using the information in the box, write your best definition of each word. Use a dictionary to check your work.

1. metamorphosis:
   change shape
2. cycle:
   in a circular pattern
3. adhere:
   to stick
4. incredible:
   not believable
5. filament:
   a thread
6. factory:
   place where things are made
7. survive:
   to live
8. construct:
   to build

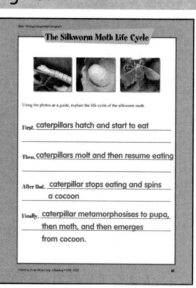

Page 67 — The Silkworm Moth Life Cycle

Using the photos as a guide, explain the life cycle of the silkworm moth.

First, caterpillars hatch and start to eat

Then, caterpillars molt and then resume eating

After that, caterpillar stops eating and spins a cocoon

Finally, caterpillar metamorphosises to pupa, then moth, and then emerges from cocoon.

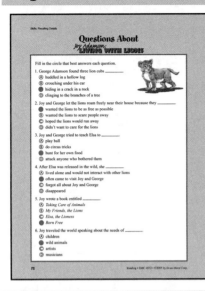

Skills: Reading Details

Questions About
Joy Adamson: LIVING WITH LIONS

Fill in the circle that best answers each question.

1. George Adamson found three lion cubs _____
   - Ⓐ huddled in a hollow log
   - Ⓑ crouching under his car
   - ● hiding in a crack in a rock
   - Ⓓ clinging to the branches of a tree

2. Joy and George let the lions roam freely near their house because they _____
   - ● wanted the lions to be as free as possible
   - Ⓑ wanted the lions to scare people away
   - Ⓒ hoped the lions would run away
   - Ⓓ didn't want to care for the lions

3. Joy and George tried to teach Elsa to _____
   - Ⓐ play ball
   - Ⓑ do circus tricks
   - ● hunt for her own food
   - Ⓓ attack anyone who bothered them

4. After Elsa was released in the wild, she _____
   - Ⓐ lived alone and would not interact with other lions
   - ● often came to visit Joy and George
   - Ⓒ forgot all about Joy and George
   - Ⓓ disappeared

5. Joy wrote a book entitled _____
   - Ⓐ Taking Care of Animals
   - Ⓑ My Friends, the Lions
   - Ⓒ Elsa, the Lioness
   - ● Born Free

6. Joy traveled the world speaking about the needs of _____
   - Ⓐ children
   - ● wild animals
   - Ⓒ artists
   - Ⓓ musicians

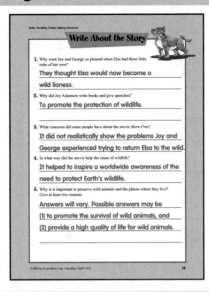

Skills: Reading Details, Making Inferences

Write About the Story

1. Why were Joy and George so pleased when Elsa had three little cubs of her own?
   They thought Elsa would now become a wild lioness.

2. Why did Joy Adamson write books and give speeches?
   To promote the protection of wildlife.

3. What concerns did some people have about the movie *Born Free*?
   It did not realistically show the problems Joy and George experienced trying to return Elsa to the wild.

4. In what way did the movie help the cause of wildlife?
   It helped to inspire a worldwide awareness of the need to protect Earth's wildlife.

5. Why is it important to preserve wild animals and the places where they live? Give at least two reasons.
   Answers will vary. Possible answers may be (1) to promote the survival of wild animals, and (2) provide a high quality of life for wild animals.

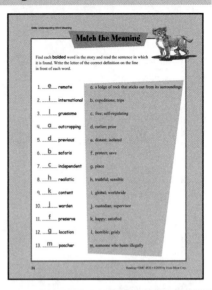

Skills: Understanding Word Meaning

Match the Meaning

Find each bolded word in the story and read the sentence in which it is found. Write the letter of the correct definition on the line in front of each word.

1. __e__ remote   a. a lodge of rock that sticks out from its surroundings
2. __i__ international   b. expeditions; trips
3. __l__ gruesome   c. free; self-regulating
4. __a__ outcropping   d. earlier; prior
5. __d__ previous   e. distant; isolated
6. __b__ safaris   f. protect; save
7. __c__ independent   g. place
8. __h__ realistic   h. truthful; sensible
9. __k__ content   i. global; worldwide
10. __j__ warden   j. custodian; supervisor
11. __f__ preserve   k. happy; satisfied
12. __g__ location   l. horrible; grisly
13. __m__ poacher   m. someone who hunts illegally

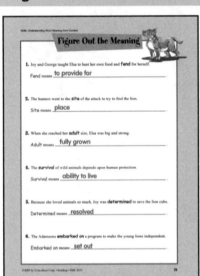

Skills: Understanding Word Meaning from Context

Figure Out the Meaning

1. Joy and George taught Elsa to hunt for her own food and **fend** for herself.
   Fend means __to provide for__

2. The hunters went to the **site** of the attack to try to find the lion.
   Site means __place__

3. When she reached her **adult** size, Elsa was big and strong.
   Adult means __fully grown__

4. The **survival** of wild animals depends upon human protection.
   Survival means __ability to live__

5. Because she loved animals so much, Joy was **determined** to save the lion cubs.
   Determined means __resolved__

6. The Adamsons **embarked on** a program to make the young lions independent.
   Embarked on means __set out__

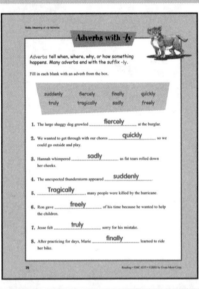

Skills: Meaning of -ly Adverbs

Adverbs with -ly

Adverbs tell when, where, why, or how something happens. Many adverbs end with the suffix -ly.

Fill in each blank with an adverb from the box.

| suddenly | fiercely | finally | quickly |
| truly | tragically | sadly | freely |

1. The large shaggy dog growled __fiercely__ at the burglar.
2. We wanted to get through with our chores __quickly__ so we could go outside and play.
3. Hannah whimpered __sadly__ as fat tears rolled down her cheeks.
4. The unexpected thunderstorm appeared __suddenly__
5. __Tragically__ many people were killed by the hurricane.
6. Ron gave __freely__ of his time because he wanted to help the children.
7. Jesse felt __truly__ sorry for his mistake.
8. After practicing for days, Marie __finally__ learned to ride her bike.

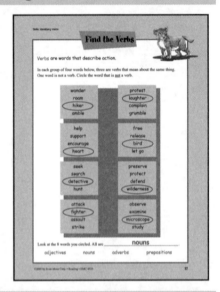

Skills: Identifying Verbs

Find the Verbs

Verbs are words that describe action.

In each group of four words below, three are verbs that mean about the same thing. One word is not a verb. Circle the word that is *not* a verb.

wonder / roam / (hiker) / amble

protest / (laughter) / complain / grumble

help / support / encourage / (heart)

free / release / (bird) / let go

seek / search / (detective) / hunt

preserve / protect / defend / (wilderness)

attack / (fighter) / assault / strike

observe / examine / (microscope) / study

Look at the 8 words you circled. All are __nouns__.
adjectives   nouns   adverbs   prepositions

Skills: Reading Details, Analyzing Character Traits, Drawing Conclusions

Questions About
OLD BRAGWYNN the PIRATE

Fill in the circle that best answers each question.

1. Which words best describe Old Bragwynn?
   - Ⓐ dastardly and villainous
   - Ⓑ delusional and nutty
   - Ⓒ capable and crafty
   - Ⓓ smart and witty

2. Which words best describe the captain?
   - Ⓐ welcoming and kindhearted
   - Ⓑ understanding and tolerant
   - Ⓒ jolly and friendly
   - Ⓓ shrewd and ruthless

3. What is a *Jolly Roger*?
   - Ⓐ a pirate flag with skull and crossbones
   - Ⓑ another way of saying "walk the plank"
   - Ⓒ the name of the pirate ship
   - Ⓓ the funniest of the pirates

4. What did Bragwynn order Jack to do?
   - Ⓐ bite the captain
   - Ⓑ howl at the moon
   - Ⓒ tie up the sailors
   - Ⓓ jump into the water

5. Where did Bragwynn think he was going when he stepped through the door?
   - Ⓐ into his new captain's quarters
   - Ⓑ back to his own boat
   - Ⓒ into the bathroom
   - Ⓓ into the kitchen

6. What became of Jack?
   - Ⓐ He jumped into the water to try to save his master.
   - Ⓑ He floated away in the rowboat.
   - Ⓒ He died of a broken heart.
   - Ⓓ He stayed on the pirate ship.

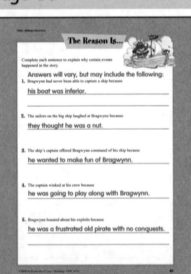

Skills: Making Inferences

The Reason Is...

Complete each sentence to explain why certain events happened in the story.

Answers will vary, but may include the following:

1. Bragwynn had never been able to capture a ship because __his boat was inferior.__

2. The sailors on the big ship laughed at Bragwynn because __they thought he was a nut.__

3. The ship's captain offered Bragwynn command of his ship because __he wanted to make fun of Bragwynn.__

4. The captain winked at his crew because __he was going to play along with Bragwynn.__

5. Bragwynn boasted about his exploits because __he was a frustrated old pirate with no conquests.__

Skills: Using Reading Word Meaning

Match the Meaning

Find each bolded word in the story and read the sentence in which it is found. Write the letter of the correct definition on the line in front of each word.

1. __c__ villain   a. housing; a place to stay
2. __b__ capsizing   b. overturning
3. __e__ surrender   c. a criminal or bad person
4. __h__ demotion   d. to make strong and steady
5. __i__ stifle   e. to give up
6. __j__ pact   f. reasoning
7. __g__ dastardly   g. mean and cruel
8. __a__ lodgings   h. a reduction in status or rank
9. __f__ logic   i. hold back; stop
10. __d__ stabilize   j. deal; agreement

Choose two of the words and use each in a sentence.
Answers will vary, but should include two words from the above list used correctly.

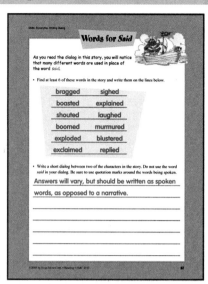

Words for Said

As you read the dialog in this story, you will notice that many different words are used in place of the word *said*.

- Find at least 6 of these words in the story and write them on the lines below.

bragged	sighed
boasted	explained
shouted	laughed
boomed	murmured
exploded	blustered
exclaimed	replied

- Write a short dialog between two of the characters in the story. Do not use the word *said* in your dialog. Be sure to use quotation marks around the words being spoken.

Answers will vary, but should be written as spoken words, as opposed to a narrative.

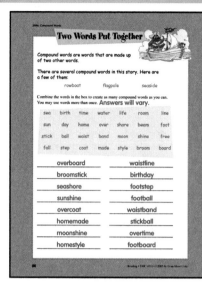

Two Words Put Together

Compound words are words that are made up of two other words.

There are several compound words in this story. Here are a few of them:

rowboat   flagpole   seaside

Combine the words in the box to create as many compound words as you can. You may use words more than once. Answers will vary.

sea	birth	time	water	life	room	line
sun	day	home	over	shore	beam	foot
stick	ball	waist	band	moon	shine	free
fall	step	coat	made	style	broom	board

overboard	waistline
broomstick	birthday
seashore	footstep
sunshine	football
overcoat	waistband
homemade	stickball
moonshine	overtime
homestyle	footboard

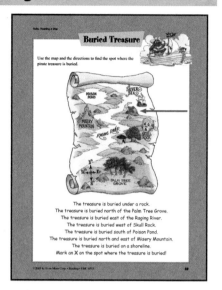

Buried Treasure

Use the map and the directions to find the spot where the pirate treasure is buried.

The treasure is buried under a rock.
The treasure is buried north of the Palm Tree Grove.
The treasure is buried east of the Raging River.
The treasure is buried west of Skull Rock.
The treasure is buried south of Poison Pond.
The treasure is buried north and east of Misery Mountain.
The treasure is buried on a shoreline.
Mark an X on the spot where the treasure is buried!

Questions About KANGAROO ALMANAC

Fill in the circle that best answers each question.

1. Kangaroos are native to which of these continents?
   - Ⓐ Asia
   - Ⓑ Europe
   - Ⓒ Antarctica
   - ● Australia

2. In which U.S. state can you find the largest collection of kangaroos outside Australia?
   - Ⓐ Iowa
   - Ⓑ New York
   - ● Georgia
   - Ⓓ California

3. Which of these is not a way kangaroos keep cool?
   - Ⓐ They pant rapidly.
   - ● They hop into a billabong.
   - Ⓒ They wet their forearms with saliva.
   - Ⓓ They dig a hole in the cool dirt under a tree.

4. Which statement tells about newborn kangaroos?
   - Ⓐ They look like jelly beans.
   - ● They are tiny and hairless.
   - Ⓒ They are born in the mother's pouch.
   - Ⓓ They are able to hop soon after birth.

5. In which way can kangaroos be dangerous to people?
   - Ⓐ They can kick and punch.
   - Ⓑ They can claw and bite.
   - ● They can knock a person over with their tails.
   - Ⓓ They can dig holes and knock down fences.

6. What is the top speed of a large kangaroo?
   - Ⓐ about 10 miles per hour
   - Ⓑ about 20 miles per hour
   - ● about 50 miles per hour
   - Ⓓ about 100 miles per hour

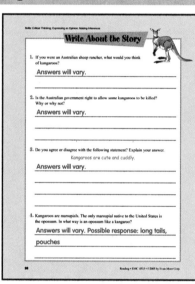

Write About the Story

1. If you were an Australian sheep rancher, what would you think of kangaroos?
   Answers will vary.

2. Is the Australian government right to allow some kangaroos to be killed? Why or why not?
   Answers will vary.

3. Do you agree or disagree with the following statement? Explain your answer.
   Kangaroos are cute and cuddly.
   Answers will vary.

4. Kangaroos are marsupials. The only marsupial native to the United States is the opossum. In what way is an opossum like a kangaroo?
   Answers will vary. Possible response: long tails, pouches

Choose the Right Meaning

Find these highlighted words in the story. Read the sentence in which each word is found. Choose the correct meaning.

1. A dingo is _____
   - Ⓐ a wild pig
   - ● a wild dog
   - Ⓒ a wild horse
   - Ⓓ a wild cat

2. The word conservation means _____
   - ● care and protection
   - Ⓑ a meeting of a group
   - Ⓒ a talk between several people
   - Ⓓ changing of water vapor to liquid water

3. A habitat is _____
   - Ⓐ a kind of clothing for animals
   - Ⓑ the covering of an animal's skin
   - Ⓒ the way a certain kind of animal moves
   - ● the environment in which a particular animal lives

4. A scrubby tree is _____
   - Ⓐ tall
   - Ⓑ dried up
   - Ⓒ dying
   - ● undersized

5. An animal in captivity would not be in _____
   - Ⓐ a zoo
   - Ⓑ a cage
   - ● a forest
   - Ⓓ a pen

6. Where might you nestle?
   - ● in your bed
   - Ⓑ on a bench
   - Ⓒ in the shower
   - Ⓓ at the gym

7. In this story, the word matures means _____
   - Ⓐ becomes ripe
   - ● acts grownup
   - Ⓒ grows to adulthood
   - Ⓓ due and payable, like a loan

8. Which word below is an antonym for shallow?
   - Ⓐ thin
   - ● deep
   - Ⓒ low
   - Ⓓ slender

9. The word unlikely means _____
   - ● improbable
   - Ⓑ disliked
   - Ⓒ not friendly
   - Ⓓ not the same

10. If there is an overpopulation of something, _____
    - ● there are not enough of the thing
    - Ⓑ the thing is too popular
    - Ⓒ the thing costs too much
    - Ⓓ there are too many of the thing

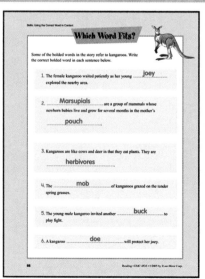

Which Word Fits?

Some of the bolded words in the story refer to kangaroos. Write the correct bolded word in each sentence below.

1. The female kangaroo waited patiently as her young **joey** explored the nearby area.

2. **Marsupials** are a group of mammals whose newborn babies live and grow for several months in the mother's **pouch**

3. Kangaroos are like cows and deer in that they eat plants. They are **herbivores**

4. The **mob** of kangaroos grazed on the tender spring grasses.

5. The young male kangaroo invited another **buck** to play fight.

6. A kangaroo **doe** will protect her joey.

Fact or Opinion?

A **fact** tells information that is true.
An **opinion** tells about someone's thoughts or feelings.

Write **fact** or **opinion** after each statement.

1. Kangaroos are cute. — opinion
2. There are many different kinds of kangaroos. — fact
3. Kangaroos live in Australia. — fact
4. Kangaroos move by hopping. — fact
5. Some kangaroos live in trees. — fact
6. People should never kill kangaroos. — opinion
7. Kangaroos are herbivores. — fact
8. Kangaroos make good pets. — opinion
9. Everyone should visit the zoo to see kangaroos. — opinion
10. Kangaroos sometimes dig holes to find water. — fact

Write one fact and one opinion of your own. Ask a family member to tell which is which.

Answers will vary.

Which Spelling Is Correct?

Circle the correct spelling for each word.

1. safty / (safety) / saftey
2. (island) / iland / islind
3. neccessary / (necessary) / necessary
4. excape / (escape) / esscape
5. (million) / milion / milliun
6. anminal / annimal / (animal)
7. suprise / surprize / (surprise)
8. immagine / amagine / (imagine)
9. diffrent / (different) / differant
10. (government) / goverment / governmant

Write sentences using the correct spellings of three words from the list above.

1. Answers will vary. Each sentence should include at least one word from the above list used
2. correctly.
3.

Page 106

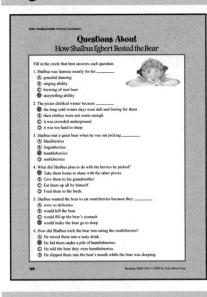

Questions About
How Shalbus Egbert Bested the Bear

Fill in the circle that best answers each question.

1. Shalbus was famous mostly for his _____
   - Ⓐ graceful dancing
   - Ⓑ singing ability
   - Ⓒ brewing of root beer
   - ● storytelling ability

2. The pixies disliked winter because _____
   - ● the long cold winter days were dull and boring for them
   - Ⓑ their clothes were not warm enough
   - Ⓒ it was crowded underground
   - Ⓓ it was too hard to sleep

3. Shalbus met a great bear when he was out picking _____
   - Ⓐ blackberries
   - Ⓑ lingonberries
   - Ⓒ bumbleberries
   - ● rootleberries

4. What did Shalbus plan to do with the berries he picked?
   - ● Take them home to share with the other pixies.
   - Ⓑ Give them to his grandmother.
   - Ⓒ Eat them up all by himself.
   - Ⓓ Feed them to the birds.

5. Shalbus wanted the bear to eat rootleberries because they _____
   - Ⓐ were so delicious
   - Ⓑ would kill the bear
   - Ⓒ would fill up the bear's stomach
   - ● would make the bear go to sleep

6. How did Shalbus trick the bear into eating the rootleberries?
   - Ⓐ He mixed them into a tasty drink.
   - Ⓑ He hid them under a pile of bumbleberries.
   - ● He told the bear they were bumbleberries.
   - Ⓓ He slipped them into the bear's mouth while the bear was sleeping.

Page 107

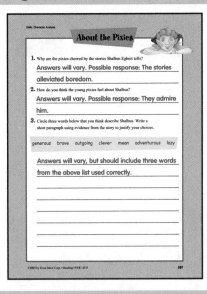

About the Pixies

1. Why are the pixies cheered by the stories Shalbus Egbert tells?
   Answers will vary. Possible response: The stories alleviated boredom.

2. How do you think the young pixies feel about Shalbus?
   Answers will vary. Possible response: They admire him.

3. Circle three words below that you think describe Shalbus. Write a short paragraph using evidence from the story to justify your choices.

   generous   brave   outgoing   clever   mean   adventurous   lazy

   Answers will vary, but should include three words from the above list used correctly.

Page 108

Choose the Right Meaning

Find these highlighted words in the story. Read the sentence in which each word is found. Choose the correct meaning.

1. The word stature means _____
   - Ⓐ monument
   - Ⓑ bridge
   - ● height
   - Ⓓ color

2. The word huddled means _____
   - Ⓐ lost
   - Ⓑ frightened
   - Ⓒ joined hands
   - ● crowded together

3. The word renegotiate means _____
   - Ⓐ to explain
   - Ⓑ to change
   - Ⓒ to convince
   - ● to bargain again

4. The word laden means _____
   - ● overloaded
   - Ⓑ cheerful
   - Ⓒ soggy
   - Ⓓ stinky

5. The word assuaged means _____
   - Ⓐ complained
   - ● satisfied
   - Ⓒ forgotten
   - Ⓓ injured

6. The word agonizing means _____
   - Ⓐ very funny
   - Ⓑ rather mild
   - ● extremely painful
   - Ⓓ somewhat embarrassing

7. The word glee means _____
   - Ⓐ sleepiness
   - Ⓑ sorrow
   - Ⓒ anger
   - ● joy

8. The word strayed means _____
   - ● wandered
   - Ⓑ leapt
   - Ⓒ crept
   - Ⓓ poured

9. The word insignificant means _____
   - Ⓐ large and beautiful
   - ● not important
   - Ⓒ shiny
   - Ⓓ soft

10. The word heap means _____
   - ● a pile
   - Ⓑ a pound
   - Ⓒ a basket
   - Ⓓ a string

Page 109

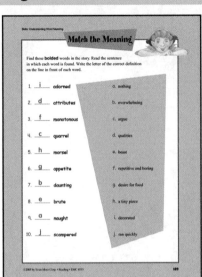

Match the Meaning

Find these bolded words in the story. Read the sentence in which each word is found. Write the letter of the correct definition on the line in front of each word.

1. **i** adorned
2. **d** attributes
3. **f** monotonous
4. **c** quarrel
5. **h** morsel
6. **g** appetite
7. **b** daunting
8. **e** brute
9. **a** naught
10. **j** scampered

   a. nothing
   b. overwhelming
   c. argue
   d. qualities
   e. beast
   f. repetitive and boring
   g. desire for food
   h. a tiny piece
   i. decorated
   j. ran quickly

Page 110

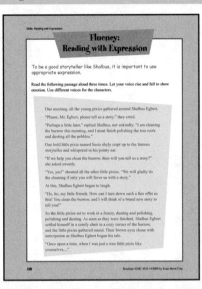

Fluency: Reading with Expression

To be a good storyteller like Shalbus, it is important to use appropriate expression.

Read the following passage aloud three times. Let your voice rise and fall to show emotion. Use different voices for the characters.

One morning, all the young pixies gathered around Shalbus Egbert.

"Please, Mr. Egbert, please tell us a story," they cried.

"Perhaps a little later," replied Shalbus, not unkindly. "I am cleaning the burrow this morning, and I must finish polishing the tree roots and dusting all the pebbles."

One bold little pixie named Susie shyly crept up to the famous storyteller and whispered in his pointy ear.

"If we help you clean the burrow, then will you tell us a story?" she asked sweetly.

"Yes, yes!" shouted all the other little pixies. "We will gladly do the cleaning if only you will favor us with a story."

At this, Shalbus Egbert began to laugh.

"Ho, ho, my little friends. How can I turn down such a fine offer as this? You clean the burrow, and I will think of a brand new story to tell you!"

So the little pixies set to work in a frenzy, dusting and polishing, polishing and dusting. As soon as they were finished, Shalbus Egbert settled himself in a comfy chair in a cozy corner of the burrow, and the little pixies gathered round. Their brown eyes shone with anticipation as Shalbus Egbert began his tale.

"Once upon a time, when I was just a wee little pixie like yourselves..."

Page 111

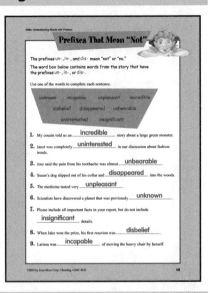

Prefixes That Mean "Not"

The prefixes un-, in-, and dis- mean "not" or "no."
The word box below contains words from the story that have the prefixes un-, in-, or dis-.

Use one of the words to complete each sentence.

   unknown   incapable   unpleasant   incredible
   disbelief   disappeared   unbearable
   uninterested   insignificant

1. My cousin told us an **incredible** story about a large green monster.
2. Janet was completely **uninterested** in our discussion about fashion trends.
3. Jose said the pain from his toothache was almost **unbearable**.
4. Susan's dog slipped out of his collar and **disappeared** into the woods.
5. The medicine tasted very **unpleasant**.
6. Scientists have discovered a planet that was previously **unknown**.
7. Please include all important facts in your report, but do not include **insignificant** details.
8. When Jake won the prize, his first reaction was **disbelief**.
9. Larissa was **incapable** of moving the heavy chair by herself.

Page 116

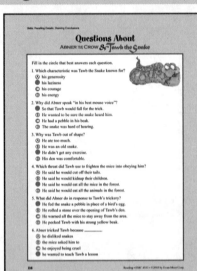

Questions About
ABNER THE CROW & Tawb the Snake

Fill in the circle that best answers each question.

1. Which characteristic was Tawb the Snake known for?
   - Ⓐ his generosity
   - ● his laziness
   - Ⓒ his courage
   - Ⓓ his energy

2. Why did Abner speak "in his best mouse voice"?
   - ● So that Tawb would fall for the trick.
   - Ⓑ He wanted to be sure the snake heard him.
   - Ⓒ He had a pebble in his beak.
   - Ⓓ The snake was hard of hearing.

3. Why was Tawb out of shape?
   - Ⓐ He ate too much.
   - Ⓑ He was an old snake.
   - ● He didn't get any exercise.
   - Ⓓ His den was comfortable.

4. Which threat did Tawb use to frighten the mice into obeying him?
   - Ⓐ He said he would cut off their tails.
   - Ⓑ He said he would kidnap their children.
   - ● He said he would eat all the mice in the forest.
   - Ⓓ He said he would eat all the animals in the forest.

5. What did Abner do in response to Tawb's trickery?
   - ● He fed the snake a pebble in place of a bird's egg.
   - Ⓑ He rolled a stone over the opening of Tawb's den.
   - Ⓒ He warned all the mice to stay away from the area.
   - Ⓓ He pecked Tawb with his strong yellow beak.

6. Abner tricked Tawb because _____
   - Ⓐ he disliked snakes
   - Ⓑ the mice asked him to
   - Ⓒ he enjoyed being tricky
   - ● he wanted to teach Tawb a lesson

Page 117

How Did They Feel?

Complete each sentence to identify the feelings of the characters in these situations. Draw a picture to illustrate each situation.

Tawb felt **clever** after successfully tricking the first mouse.	The first mouse felt **terrified** when confronting Tawb.
Answers may vary.	
Abner felt **disgust** as he observed Tawb's actions.	The second mouse felt **grateful** when Abner told him to run.

Page 118

Choose the Right Meaning

Find these highlighted words in the story. Read the sentence in which each word is found. Choose the correct meaning.

1. The word ancient means extremely _____
   - ● old
   - Ⓑ pretty
   - Ⓒ worried
   - Ⓓ dangerous

2. The word stammer means _____
   - Ⓐ cough and choke
   - Ⓑ shout or speak loudly
   - ● stutter or speak haltingly
   - Ⓓ whisper or speak quietly

3. The word evident means _____
   - Ⓐ strange
   - ● obvious
   - Ⓒ confusing
   - Ⓓ mysterious

4. The word sensation means _____
   - Ⓐ fur
   - Ⓑ view
   - Ⓒ belief
   - ● feeling

5. The word pleasant means _____
   - ● enjoyable
   - Ⓑ painful
   - Ⓒ nasty
   - Ⓓ dark

6. The word bargain means _____
   - Ⓐ pen
   - ● deal
   - Ⓒ catalog
   - Ⓓ wheelbarrow

7. The word proposition means _____
   - Ⓐ lie
   - Ⓑ order
   - ● proposal
   - Ⓓ demand

8. The word intercepted means _____
   - Ⓐ punished
   - ● stopped on the way
   - Ⓒ sneaked up on
   - Ⓓ pretended to be interested

9. The word stealthily means _____
   - Ⓐ shyly
   - Ⓑ carefully
   - Ⓒ anxiously
   - ● secretly

10. The word gullet means _____
   - Ⓐ thrust
   - Ⓑ tunnel
   - ● tongue
   - Ⓓ cheek

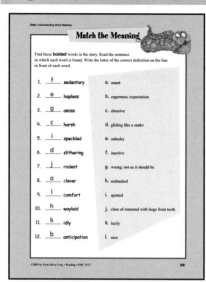

Page 119 — Match the Meaning

Skills: Understanding Word Meaning

Find these **bolded** words in the story. Read the sentence in which each word is found. Write the letter of the correct definition on the line in front of each word.

1. f sedentary
2. e hapless
3. g amiss
4. c harsh
5. i speckled
6. d slithering
7. j rodent
8. a clever
9. l comfort
10. h waylaid
11. k idly
12. b anticipation

a. smart
b. eagerness; expectation
c. abrasive
d. gliding like a snake
e. unlucky
f. inactive
g. wrong; not as it should be
h. ambushed
i. spotted
j. class of mammal with large front teeth
k. lazily
l. ease

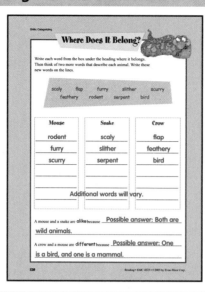

Page 120 — Where Does It Belong?

Skills: Categorizing

Write each word from the box under the heading where it belongs. Then think of two more words that describe each animal. Write these new words on the lines.

scaly   flap   furry   slither   scurry
feathery   rodent   serpent   bird

Mouse	Snake	Crow
rodent	scaly	flap
furry	slither	feathery
scurry	serpent	bird

Additional words will vary.

A mouse and a snake are alike because Possible answer: Both are wild animals.

A crow and a mouse are different because Possible answer: One is a bird, and one is a mammal.

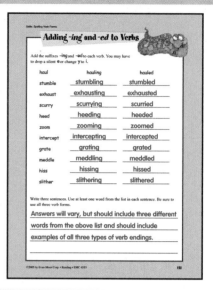

Page 121 — Adding -ing and -ed to Verbs

Skills: Spelling Verb Forms

Add the suffixes -ing and -ed to each verb. You may have to drop a silent e or change y to i.

haul	hauling	hauled
stumble	stumbling	stumbled
exhaust	exhausting	exhausted
scurry	scurrying	scurried
heed	heeding	heeded
zoom	zooming	zoomed
intercept	intercepting	intercepted
grate	grating	grated
meddle	meddling	meddled
hiss	hissing	hissed
slither	slithering	slithered

Write three sentences. Use at least one word from the list in each sentence. Be sure to use all three verb forms.

Answers will vary, but should include three different words from the above list and should include examples of all three types of verb endings.

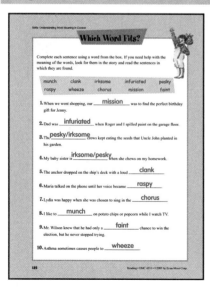

Page 129 — Questions About Shiver & Quake

Skills: Recalling Details; Making Inferences

Fill in the circle that best answers each question.

1. The boy felt bad because he
   Ⓐ had no money
   Ⓑ didn't want to work
   ● spent all his time daydreaming
   Ⓓ caused his parents to worry

2. The robber did not try to steal from the boy because he
   Ⓐ wanted the boy to go to the haunted house
   ● could tell that the boy had no possessions
   Ⓒ was afraid of the boy
   Ⓓ liked the boy

3. The boy stuffed his ears with rags because the
   Ⓐ ghoul wheezed too loudly
   Ⓑ ogre's roars hurt his ears
   Ⓒ sizzle of the fire kept him awake
   ● goblins' shrieks were so annoying

4. On the third morning, the boy awoke to find
   ● the house and its surroundings were now lovely
   Ⓑ all the spooky creatures had returned
   Ⓒ his bread had been eaten by mice
   Ⓓ the hollow voice laughing at him

5. What caused the spell on the house to be broken?
   ● the boy's lack of fear
   Ⓑ the creatures burned up
   Ⓒ the robber cast a new spell
   Ⓓ the time of the spell was up

6. What did the boy do with the trunks of gold?
   Ⓐ He put them under the bed.
   ● He stacked them in the cellar.
   Ⓒ He buried them in the garden.
   Ⓓ He took them to his parents.

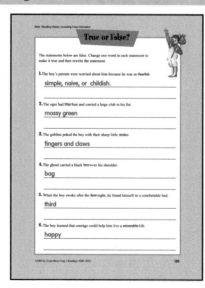

Page 130 — Write About the Story

Skills: Critical Thinking; Expressing an Opinion

Some people might say the boy in this story was silly and not very bright. Others might disagree with this statement. What do you think? Defend your position with events from the story.

Answers will vary, but the opinion should be supported by facts from the story that reinforce the chosen point of view.

Page 131 — Choose the Right Meaning

Skills: Understanding Word Meaning

Find these highlighted words in the story. Read the sentence in which each word is found. Choose the correct meaning.

1. Which of these would be a **disappointment**?
   Ⓐ new toys
   Ⓑ a surprise party
   ● losing the championship
   Ⓓ winning the state lottery

2. The word **gusto** in this story means
   ● enthusiasm and enjoyment
   Ⓑ sadness and longing
   Ⓒ pain and suffering
   Ⓓ fear and dread

3. The word **pluck** in this story means
   Ⓐ fancy clothes
   ● confidence
   Ⓒ wealth
   Ⓓ voice

4. The word **shrill** describes a sound that is
   Ⓐ soft and melodic
   Ⓑ deep and rumbling
   Ⓒ muffled and rhythmic
   ● high-pitched and piercing

5. The word **awkwardly** means about the same as
   Ⓐ gracefully
   ● clumsily
   Ⓒ nimbly
   Ⓓ quickly

6. Which of these could not be described as **massive**?
   ● a twig
   Ⓑ a boulder
   Ⓒ a tree trunk
   Ⓓ an elephant

7. When might you **shriek** with delight?
   Ⓐ when you see a scary movie
   Ⓑ when you stub your toe
   ● when you get a new bicycle
   Ⓓ when a friend jumps out and says "boo"

8. A house that is **gloomy** is
   Ⓐ friendly looking
   Ⓑ brightly lit
   ● dark
   Ⓓ old

9. Which word is a synonym for **bounded**?
   Ⓐ sat down
   Ⓑ tied up
   Ⓒ ran off
   ● jumped

10. How would you move if you **clambered** up the stairs?
   ● clumsily
   Ⓑ on tiptoe
   Ⓒ one step at a time
   Ⓓ by leaps and bounds

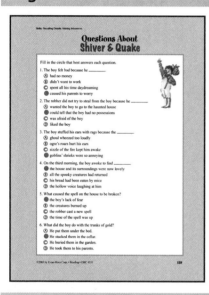

Page 132 — Which Word Fits?

Skills: Understanding Word Meaning in Context

Complete each sentence using a word from the box. If you need help with the meaning of the words, look for them in the story and read the sentences in which they are found.

munch   clank   irksome   infuriated   pesky
raspy   wheeze   chorus   mission   faint

1. When we went shopping, our mission was to find the perfect birthday gift for Jenny.
2. Dad was infuriated when Roger and I spilled paint on the garage floor.
3. The pesky/irksome crows kept eating the seeds that Uncle John planted in his garden.
4. My baby sister is irksome/pesky when she chews on my homework.
5. The anchor dropped on the ship's deck with a loud clank.
6. Maria talked on the phone until her voice became raspy.
7. Lydia was happy when she was chosen to sing in the chorus.
8. I like to munch on potato chips or popcorn while I watch TV.
9. Mr. Wilson knew that he had only a faint chance to win the election, but he never stopped trying.
10. Asthma sometimes causes people to wheeze.

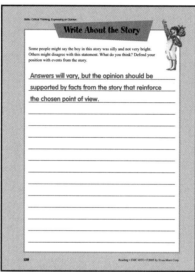

Page 133 — True or False?

Skills: Recalling Details; Correcting False Information

The statements below are false. Change one word in each statement to make it true and then rewrite the statement.

1. The boy's parents were worried about him because he was so ~~fearful~~.
   simple, naive, or childish.

2. The ogre had ~~blue~~ hair and carried a large club in his fist.
   mossy green

3. The goblins poked the boy with their sharp little ~~sticks~~.
   fingers and claws

4. The ghoul carried a black ~~hat~~ over his shoulder.
   bag

5. When the boy awoke after the ~~first~~ night, he found himself in a comfortable bed.
   third

6. The boy learned that courage could help him live a ~~miserable~~ life.
   happy

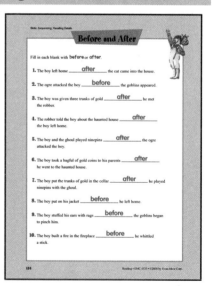

Page 134 — Before and After

Skills: Sequencing; Recalling Details

Fill in each blank with before or after.

1. The boy left home after the cat came into the house.
2. The ogre attacked the boy before the goblins appeared.
3. The boy was given three trunks of gold after he met the robber.
4. The robber told the boy about the haunted house after the boy left home.
5. The boy and the ghoul played ninepins after the ogre attacked the boy.
6. The boy took a bagful of gold coins to his parents after he went to the haunted house.
7. The boy put the trunks of gold in the cellar after he played ninepins with the ghoul.
8. The boy put on his jacket before he left home.
9. The boy stuffed his ears with rags before the goblins began to pinch him.
10. The boy built a fire in the fireplace before he whittled a stick.

Reading • EMC 4533 • ©2005 by Evan-Moor Corp.